Oh Canada, My Canada
Impressions of an Alien Son

Once you've read me, please
pass me on.
Thanks
Pud

National Library of Canada Cataloguing in Publication Data

Smith, John Ronald, 1939-
    Oh Canada, my Canada

    ISBN 1-55212-706-0

    1. Indians of North America--Cultural assimilation--
Canada.   2.
Canada--Social conditions.   3. Indians of North
America--Colonization--Canada.   4. Canada--Civilization--
British
influences.* I. Title.
E78.C2S624 2001   917'.00497   C2001-910569-X

TRAFFORD

This book was published *on-demand* in cooperation with Trafford Publishing.
On-demand publishing is a unique process and service of making a book available for retail sale to the public taking advantage of on-demand manufacturing and Internet marketing.
On-demand publishing includes promotions, retail sales, manufacturing, order fulfilment, accounting and collecting royalties on behalf of the author.

Suite 6E, 2333 Government St., Victoria, B.C. V8T 4P4, CANADA
Phone   250-383-6864   Toll-free   1-888-232-4444 (Canada & US)
Fax   250-383-6804   E-mail   sales@trafford.com
Web site   www.trafford.com   TRAFFORD PUBLISHING IS A DIVISION OF TRAFFORD HOLDINGS LTD.
Trafford Catalogue #01-0105   www.trafford.com/robots/01-0105.html

10   9   8   7   6   5   4

Oh Canada, My Canada
Impressions of an Alien Son

JOHN RONALD (PUD) SMITH

It's not *always* in a name, is it Pearl?

The name I was given, for example, is John Smith, a fine English name, would you agree? I am, however, hardly English. Some would say I'm a composite person with origins in three continents, being of African, North American Indian and Scottish heritage.

I prefer to think of myself as someone who is supremely privileged to have the experience of citizenship in two countries —naturalized in Canada and born in the States—the son of a Canadian man and an American woman. The Scottish roots in our Canadian ancestry trace back to the mid 1600s and who knows how deep our Indian roots go? My older sibling and I were raised in a Canadian city and my early life experience was Canadian, which is what this is about: my Canada.

In my Canadian experience a quiet form of racism has been as constant in the way we live as denial that Canada's still very much a British colony is in the way Canadians exist.

History confirms that colonialism and racism are synonymous. When the European savage stole a country, prominent among institutions installed by this conqueror-thief was systemic racism. In that regard the Canada that was taken from people who initially welcomed their "visitors" has changed only in the way it appears from the outside. Once you slip inside you'll experience a different story altogether.

It's my belief—and a true hope—that we can live harmoniously after we free ourselves of our prejudices and our unhealthy attachment to colonial ways. Before that can happen, however, people need to come out of the shadows and acknowledge that toxic social conditions exist. I personally carry strong feelings about seeing Canada purged of the British colonial influence, something that's been growing in me since I became consciously aware of the powerful effect that influence exerts on people. When the awareness focuses that one's life experience, perceptions and belief systems have been influenced by someone else's story I think it would be a missed opportunity to not engage seriously in learning more about the story before breaking free of its effects.

You can be pretty sure that any living creature that's controlled by another entity from exercising its own identity will most likely receive its sense of meaning from the entity that's controlling it. And it's as certain as dark clouds that if you allow yourself to be defined by someone other than yourself you can spend your forever seeking your identity and never fulfilling who you are. To not have authorship of one's life positions that person to become prey to people who operate power systems like school, the work place, religion, government...

There are so many good souls I'm grateful to, beginning with the older generation that shared their life understanding—thanks for lovely memories—and ending with folks who took time away from their own passions to support me in doing this. Thank you, Owen Ball. Thank you for you, my dear Wayne State University English teacher and lasting friend N. Catherine Collie. Thank you Carol Talbot for your insightful criticism, suggestions and encouragement. Thanks Craig Anderson for hangin' with me man, never judging, always supporting and bringing into focus the meaning of friendship. I am most privileged to know gentle Shannon Buchan, who possesses the same good-heart qualities. And Vito Dunford, the epitome of what a Canadian male can be. Joe, you know. Jess, you bad. Billy-bud, Canada needs more folks like you. Thank you, Lynda Raino, for who you are and what you release in me when we exchange thoughts, ideas and the understanding of our experiences. A special thanks to my niece and godchild, Mrs. Cheryl Ann Baxter, who put my efforts into perspective. My sons Jesse B. and Beau D. Smith are an inspiration and every reason in the world to cherish the gift of fatherhood. To all who tolerated my process, thank you.

I dedicate this writing to my first son, Mr. Gregory Alan Smith, who chose death nine days after his twenty-fourth birthday.

$\int$ome years ago I read *I Ain't Much Baby, But I'm All I Got* and I was deeply moved by author Jess Lair's compassion surrounding the thoughtless destruction of South African Zulu culture.

Dr. Lair indicated that within that extraordinary culture was a most extraordinary joining of people through love. For example, when a Zulu child was born that precious gift was placed onto Mother's bare skin where the infant suckled and continued to nurse for its first few years, nurtured by Mother's love. Mother either carried her little person in her arms or the baby rode securely in a carrying sling across Mom's back. After several years the child, filled to the brim with the stuff that love produces, was released to become another good someone in the tribe. Yes indeed, to stand upright and to be universally loved. It seemed that love permeated the tribal environment and Zulu children were innocent of violence as well as of hate feelings.

The Zulu lifeway was ruthlessly redirected, however, when Zulu people were put upon by criminal-minded invaders from Europe, savages who arrived with visions of conquest and the latest in killing technology. Zulu lands were stolen from them and Zulu people were no longer allowed to live off the land. Their freedoms were caged and they came under strict control of their conquerors. Adult males were forced to leave their villages and live in squalid townships outside of cities where they were forced to accept undignified tasks that delivered substandard rewards. After eight years a man's wife was permitted to join him and, like her man, she was made to do work that the conqueror felt was below a conqueror's station. Between them a Zulu couple couldn't earn enough and the Zulu lifestyle slipped into decay. With the mothers and fathers gone Zulu homesteads became human waste lands and the people found themselves concentrated in abominable "townships." What then became of their precious children? With the adults forced into urban servitude the children were left pretty much unattended in a degrading, devaluing, depressing environment. The result was delinquency, crime and violence. A beautiful culture built on love was destroyed and the world came to hear the word and cover its eyes to the meaning of "apartheid."

Kanada

During all but the first few of my early years I endured feelings of shame, shame arising like an odor from being raised on McDougall Street in Windsor, Ontario. This, even though my father was a respected man of modest means in our community and that within the boundaries of that tiny speck on the planet I was highly valued.

This gentle but troubled spirit who was my father was also a fairly influential individual, a catalyst pursued for personal benefit by mayors and others who didn't personally care the width of a dog hair about him. As it happened he owned a place in the community that could influence a mayor's day but he was really none of the person who would think to do so. He was simply a good man who suffered with the relentless frustrations that accrue from having faithfully taken out a subscription to the equality lie. And he didn't entertain so much as a kindergartner's interest in political things.

Our people contended with two forms of shame I can think of. We lived with the imported shame George the Sixth, King of England put on us about who we were under British rule, and also the home-grown shame that grew out of being assigned a place that was not our choice in the British class system.

Today when I look back at our community the way people look back at their lives I see the markings of a township, a ghetto or reserve, I see where the community met conditions that characterize those institutions. I couldn't see it when I lived there because I was *inside* of it and when do you ever get a full view of anything from inside? It requires an inner understanding and an unimpaired view from outside to complete the picture.

Looking back I see that we were surrounded by a population that didn't mirror me, one that if I looked into it I couldn't see myself in. It was also a population that practiced subtle but definite ways of keeping us on the outside. Held as strangers, our opportunities for growth were restricted by the deprivation of information, through the absence of facilities and institutions that could enable us to improve our status. In the end we were most effectively controlled by economic means—assigned substandard tasks offering inadequate rewards. A translation in simple English terms? "Well, by Jove, Old Boy, you're welcome to live in our neighborhoods, to enroll your children in our schools and to join our country clubs but, by George, we control your ability to advance and well, you don't quite qualify." The truth was that even if you did qualify economically the country club doors weren't open to but a select few, none of whom looked like you.

The few from our class who did prosper were those who got out and there were still others who developed a deeper understanding that enabled them to overcome beliefs designed to render us incapable of accomplishing. Still, there were more fifty year old shoeshine "boys" and hotel bell "hops" than there were doctors (2) or lawyers (1) in our ranks. Both doctors served our community and our lawyer worked for the city because there was no way James Watson could get a fair shake practicing among his Law Society colleagues. Dr. Ken Rock and Dr. Othello P. Chatters were relatively harmless to the system. Mr. Watson, however, was a potential for challenge to an Old Boys establishment that used the law with conviction to keep us in our place. My father contended that, unlike the practicing healers, Mr. Watson didn't dare come to our aid because exercising his earned right to practice law would have seen him ultimately cast as a failure within his tribe. Another hero put back in his place. The feeling was that James Watson, Q.C. would have gotten cuckolded seventeen different ways by men who *were* the judicial system for having the audacity to seek equal treatment within the judicial system, exactly as he would have in pre-Mandela South Africa. Where he was expected to talk like his colleagues, to dress like them and to act like one of them he was denied full privileges that enabled him to *be* one of them.

What would it be like today, Donald Edward, if people of that generation hadn't been disabled from challenging the system's rulers? Suppose James Watson's stance had been, "I have no desire to talk like you, nor do I wish to dress or act like you; I'm quite pleased being myself, thank you. And I'm claiming my full share of those privileges you're keeping from me, my friend."

Much of who we believe we are is rooted in where we're from and if we've been lodged in a repressive environment it would be an extraordinary accomplishment to be anything other than the product of that environment. Like a goldfish. Leave a goldfish to spend its life contained inside a little glass bowl and you can bet all your booty that fish will remain goldfish-small and die young. Release that little living thing into a larger place and what happens? If it lives in big water Nature sees it become a fully grown carp.

The majority of our goldfish remained trapped by systemic "circumstance." A disproportionate number became lodged in jail cells and would it be surprising that some were incarcerated based on who they were? Or were not. Or were made to be. Others developed relationships with escape substances. Too many—count them, McDougall Street—expired prematurely and for some of *those* departing souls death was relief from living.

What was most harmful in this? That we—generations of people playing our parts in the oppression game—*accepted* our respective positions in relationship to each other and in relationship to ourselves.

McDougall Street

McDougall Street was a community that lived within itself during the nineteen forties and fifties when I grew up on McDougall Street. Today that community would be seen as a study in diversity; it was populated essentially by people who were not acceptable by mainstream standards—the inequitably educated, immigrants, a sprinkling of French Canadians, a North American Indian family, people of mixed heritage and "Negroes."

Being separated from the mainstream, McDougall Street's residents developed support systems and a cultural identity that's unique within subcultures that become outriggers of the dominant population. In other words, people who are made alien by the dominant culture develop their own ways and thank the Power that Is for that. Today I'm convinced that being kept apart, not allowed into White Anglo Saxon Canada as a part of the constipated whole was actually a blessing, making us relatively unaffected by conduct expectations that bound White Anglo Saxon Canada around the clock.

Populated by good souls who simply accepted one another there was openness in how we related; there was respect within our generation for a guy's rights to express and to simply be thee. As beloved Percy Walls, an automotive factory worker who moved into the city from rural Puce was known to say in his down-home way, "Biggety, folks can run their mouths but they can't run your business." In that statement, which I heard when just a sprinkle of a lad, there was everlasting meaning. To me it reinforced the understanding that you are who you are and the person whom you truly are can't be compromised.

Except for a few families, most made neighborhood kids welcome in their homes, sharing what they had, which wasn't always a whole lot, and making us part of their lifestyle. The older couple who lived next door, for example, I called "Uncle" Albert and "Aunt" Rosie Timbers. Aunt Rosie fixed anticipation taste-goodies especially for me or she scrambled eggs like no one else on this planet and when that gracious couple sat down to a simple supper there was always a place for me. After dinner Uncle Albert and I played several games of cards, usually Casino, and we sipped tea from clear glass mugs. I couldn't possibly have known then how important those few evening hours spread out over the years would be in developing respect for my homefolks. At that time in my life it was simply good time with people I loved in my heart, the folks next door who shared values and wisdom that institutions can't teach.

A man of habit, Uncle Albert methodically rolled a day's supply of cigarettes, packing them tidily into a blue Edgeworth tobacco tin, getting himself together for tomorrow. He had labored long and faithfully to purchase their home from the banking system, riding the same old beat-up bicycle to a job in the brickyard every workday, stopping occasionally at the Walker House for a brew before heading home. To Aunt Rosie, raised in a place of few possessions, their borrowed bit of Canada was the Center of Life and that they shared their lifestyle with the little rascal next door transcended a mere gesture of love. But that was how McDougall Street was.

Being raised with the belief that it was our heritage to exist under inequities of the times spared us the misdirection and the pressure that compel people to achieve materially rather than to develop spiritually. Unlike the population that controlled their destiny, McDougall Street individuals accepted one another simply for who they were, no more, no less. The shame feelings that came down like spinal chills when I ventured outside McDougall Street had no power when we were among ourselves in our home surroundings. We were generous and caring and linked by love and because our men were denied access to the process of acquiring we weren't pulled into its traps. With this I'm reminded that cultural anthropologist Dr. Joseph Schaeffer once remarked, in sharing impressions of people he had lived among in a "developing" country: "They don't have much but they're not sick," the good doctor had observed.

My parents owned the Walker House hotel, which our family of four lived in and within our lives there circulated an assortment of people who weren't caught up in fairy tales, myths or superficial games. These people—permanent roomers, employees and patrons—were my extended family. They were individuals who interacted according to who they were, doing none of that condescending goo-goo, gaa-gaa shit adults seem disposed to ladle onto little people.

On the hotel's second floor where our family apartment was located there also lived four aging men and Lewis Joseph Ford, a fine one-eyed Englishman who did the noon to four bartending shift following a full morning putting the Walker House's four drinking rooms into a clean and orderly fashion. Because the law stipulated that single men and single women be separated there were drinking rooms for men only—the Men's Bar and the Men's

Beverage Room and one for women only and I don't recall that we called that room the "Women's Beverage Room." Because men weren't allowed to sit or socialize in the women only section and women weren't allowed in the men's beverage room or bar room, if a woman and a man wanted to sit together they went into a larger room that was designated Ladies and Escorts. In the room for ladies and escorts there was a juke box that played for a nickel per play. An eight-ounce glass of beer cost a dime. The law was strict in ensuring that these rules were enforced and Lewie's job keeping those places right provided a mass of next-day messages about what the previous night had been like in each zone as well as indicators pointing to the sexual movements of Venus and Mars.

Lewie was always my special friend. Never interested in driving a car, he walked. And when there was a passel o' goods to be picked up out came his Radio Flyer wagon, which he loaded me into. Once I toppled out of that fast-moving vehicle and Lewie, whose mind may have been cultivating positive thoughts somewhere out there in headspace, somehow didn't register the soft th-*lmmp!* when my little form tumbled to Earth. Mr. Ford continued briskly along believing I was tucked safely in with the spuds and sundries. After raising my surprised self off the sidewalk I wandered into Charlie Nall's yard and was savoring a glass of Mrs. Nall's good iced tea while Mr. Nall got on the phone to my parents, wondering, "How'd your boy get in my yard, Ronnie?"

Lewis Ford was one of five Walker House roomers who revealed themselves in their own unique way.

The first, Mr. McTavish, was a drab-dressing rat of a man who walked stooped forward like he was about to lunge face-straight through a maze of old spider webs. The old bentbody was a hermit-like creature, keeping himself removed from everyone like he feared people could peep his thoughts about little girls. Although he *appeared* dirty Mr. McTavish wasn't dirty at all; he spent a nominal amount of time washing his sneaky self, which was the time I tried talking to him because an invitation into his gloomy habitat wasn't happening. Since the roomer's bathroom door didn't lock I could occasionally innocent my way in in the way that little people do, only to be mumbled at or ignored while the rat shaved his stubble face. Even with his non-communicating way Mr. McTavish communicated information about life from his unique perspective, proving there *is* something to be gained from nothing.

A second gent, referred to as "The Sheriff" for reasons I never cared to find out, was a threatening, sinister somebody who seriously guarded privacy that meant nothing outside of himself. Sheriff wasn't someone to be trifled with and I was scared right down to my ankles by that man, too scared of him to even say "Hello Mister Sheriff." It seemed to me that he hated everything about life and wished bad tidings upon anyone who wasn't miserable and nasty like he was.

Outfitted in a funeral attitude, he wore a dark vest, a subdued white shirt, black suit with creaseless trousers, a grey wide-brim and if for some reason he smiled I just knew that hardened face would crack like sidewalk cement. A stiffness in Sheriff's left leg caused him to drag a dead foot and use a rubber-tipped cane, the combination of wooden cane and decommissioned foot echoing an eerie *thmp-sshhh* in the dim corridor to his room.

Sharing a wall with my room was white-haired George Campbell's tranquil space, where I was welcomed like the kid next door. Sometimes the dignified gentle man and the curious child played long penny poker sessions, communicating in ways that didn't request words. There was a plaintive quiet in Mr. Campbell's soft voice and earnest, direct clarity in his watery blue eyes. He said little about himself but it was evident that he was one among the many who had bought into the bullshit about King and Country, had obediently gone away to fight in the Second World War and had gotten royally fucked.

Mr. Campbell never complained and were it not for the many hours two compatible spirits shared it's unlikely I would have known Mr. Campbell was alive, for George Campbell was little more than a remnant, a cancelled spirit existing in a shell that breathed in and breathed out.

Down the hall from Mr. Campbell lived Gregory Garuk, whom my father berated behind his back. He labeled Mr. Garuk a "parasite" because Mr. Garuk lived off the Canadian government and had the audacity to be critical of the Canadian government, the assumption being that Mr. Garuk should have been grateful beyond words. Also, Mr. Garuk was a foreigner. Lewis Ford affectionately called that foreign bastard an old "Bolshevik" and a "Communist," neither of which impacted me; I knew those civilized Europeans were friends, the kind of friends who couldn't possibly attack one another with words, gestures or actions.

Comrade Garuk, with a level gaze that looked into you, was born in the late 1800s Soviet Union. The man knew things you could be assured other people couldn't fathom. He read relentlessly, was a gifted wood craftsman and accomplished in communicating in multiple languages that he spoke through a silverin Lenin goatee. To preserve delicate strands of thinning fine hair he wore one of those snug fur hats and his winter overcoat weighed more than a load of fish.

Mr. Garuk's door stayed open wide, even when he was away

on his daily walk, and I never felt less than warmly appreciated in the room that contained the old Bolshevik's worldly possessions. Among his belongings, a large glass jug of home-pickled herring & onions that could get a little person's mouth watering with the thought. Sometimes the comrade opened his jug; at others lusting on the taste of herring wasn't a consideration, especially when Mr. Garuk opened the telling of stories about his motherland and the obscene acts happening there during those awful years leading into 1945. Far from a parasite in my eyes, Comrade Garuk was a cherished gift in my life.

Sheriff died in bed alone and I didn't miss his nasty ways in the least, particularly since the person who moved into his room was Breece Brooks.

Breece was a delightful spirit, a thickly built basic beer drinker with a penchant for having spirited long conversations with his very closest friend, Mr. Breece Brooks. Yo, who loves you most and who knows you best, Mr. Brooks?

There was not a hair growing out of a richly sheened scalp nor a tooth anywhere in his head and I remember my mother laughing that Breece could gum an apple or a steak to death.

You had to be alert around Breece when he became animated because the man couldn't talk without flapping a spray that made you stand back or risk getting spit-faced. I didn't care in the least about that. I loved everything about Mr. Brooks because what you got was who he was, spit or not.

Many nights I'd creep up and giggle outside the old gent's doorway while he sat with the light out in front of his window overlooking McDougall Street, talking to his best friend and worst critic. "I ain't nothin' but a damn fool, drinkin' an' gettin' drunk all the damn time," he might begin and his other self invariably

19

piped in. "Yeah, an' you always *bin* a damn fool, too. That's why you ain't got no money."

"Yeah, I know. An' people take what I don't drink up."

"You *give* 'em your damn money, fool. They don't *have* to take it."

"An' they use me, too."

"Yeah, you ain't nothin' but a damn fool."

When he discovered me Breece invariably drew me into his world. I loved the way he said my name during those times and even today the little boy in me warms with memories of the way he accepted me, that the quality of our relationship sourced in respect. In my eyes Mr. Brooks was a great man who didn't need to be called "Mr." Brooks to be great.

Gentle Breece sometimes sat through the entire night passionately chastising himself, lip-launching saliva satellites while his hairless head bounced headlight flashes from passing cars, but he was known to rarely miss a day toiling on the city's garbage trucks.

The nearby Salvation Army yard, a source of supply and adventure, was where the first authentic American bigot blended into my relationship with life. Looking back, it's not surprising that the first *recognizable* racist was American; Americans of that time were as bold with their racism as they were with their bombs and bullets. Canadians were decidedly different, operating so effectively with subtlety and denial that if you didn't have your ear to the tracks you wouldn't believe a train was coming.

We kids regarded Eddy contemptuously because Eddy had taken on the job of keeping us out of that coveted yard, which we prized for the reward of being able to make off with choice items before they reached the Salvation Army Thrift Store. Especially during the years after WWII when wives were making their returning hero husbands get rid of war souvenirs that were for them reminders of a time they preferred to forget.

Eddy looked like an ostrich-necked thing you might see in children's illustrations. Wearing ponderous work boots, suspendered work britches and one of those dull red cotton shirts, Eddy was different from what you'd normally see walking around in a factory town like Windsor. His mouth ruminating on air, he drawled in a Deep South voice, "Ain' gon be no mo' Mista Nigga, ain' gon be no mo' Mista Coon. Nosuh. We gon hang 'im up with barbwire an' kill 'im up gooood. Yessuh," and Eddy's jaundiced head would be bobbing like he was messed up on holy water.

We threw stones at Eddy, keeping a safe distance because the man could zing some rocks himself. We teased, taunted and mimicked him over the years, assuming that he would forever be available for our sport. But then one day old Eddy died.

The first kid I hooked up with (and the first to call me nigger to my face) was a carrot-topped French Canadian named Paul Gosselin, who became a forever friend after we realized that fighting, which we did a lot of in the beginning, wouldn't bring us closer together.

We were a highly visible pair—freckled Paul with his "red" hair, and beige me with a wild head of brown curls—during excursions into places where adults rarely noticed us, essentially because we had learned the art of being present without being noticed, like little trees in a tall forest. Consequently we got away with a whole lot of shit right under adult noses and there was nothing we were unwilling to try so long as the activity would make a heart jump. We were successful because we focused on the movement of what we were doing, with little thought about outcome. As we saw matters we either could or we couldn't and we wouldn't know one way or the other until we put ourselves into it. And what we did mainly was mess with people. When we ambushed evening strollers with barrages of expired produce collected from garbage drums around the City Farmer's Market our escape route mated to a detailed knowledge of the terrain, which bordered our neighborhood. Crouched like bandits in shadows, we waited for unsuspecting pedestrians to pass by and then filled the night sky with high arcing tomatoes, oranges, apples, grapefruits, sticky pears… As the garbage we put up rained silently down through the night air we were dissolving into shadows, allowing one brief, gloating pause to observe before we blended with the night.

Daytime attacks were entirely different. Sometimes we fished out used prophylactics flushed directly into a sewage system that emptied filth into the Detroit River, filled them to capacity with that fouled water and dropped the wobbling vile things off downtown rooftops. By the time people on the sidewalk below recovered from the initial shock we had hurried down a rear fire escape, walked around front like nothing had happened and quietly mixed with spectators attracted to the spectacle. A coupla times, though, we were surprised by people in the alley and had to bust our jets in the opposite direction.

Once in a rare while we made off with a full crate of eggs from Silverwood's Dairy warehouse and stashed it in open sunlight on a downtown roof. It was from that hiding-place that we took our supplies and hurled waves of eggs off other downtown roofs. Or from strategic alley positions we sprang into a line of throwers who unleashed a storm through the open windows of moving city buses, which weren't air conditioned during that period in Windsor's history. That adventure in throwing was the ultimate because we were free to cut loose at full power and get instant gratification from seeing the effects of those flying yolk bombs. Personally, I got a much bigger charge from splashing an egg up the side of someone's shoulder than I did lobbing fruit up and waiting for it to come down. And throwing eggs was infinitely less dangerous than bouncing a rock off someone's noggin. As I recall, there were more than a few strong arms that prized splattering bus riders above all other throwing adventures. But we were limited to rare appearances because splattering a bus load of people got all of officialdom stirred up and put pressure on cops who'd grab you just to let you know who was in control.

One night we egg-bombed a three-wheeler motorcycle cop who had stopped on red at an intersection, maybe seventy or so feet from an alley we had set up in.

Paul and I had agreed never to bunch up because bunching facilitated getting nabbed, tagged and put in storage. A slower runner than I, the French Canadian kid usually took flight first. My arrogance contributed to the arrangement; I believed myself uncatchable, a kind of mystic spirit who could smile at danger and dance away laughing.

We cut loose with a barrage that went up on a high arcing line, rounded downward at its zenith and sliced silently earthward at accelerating speed. I heard Paul make his quick exit but kept watching, knowing the police officer was a blink away from a new experience, thinking *Catch me if you can, buddy*. When the barrage splattered all over that black-clad symbol of authority and his shiny high-powered bike I figured the guy would be shocked, buying me time to sprint away unseen.

The man reacted instantly. Slamming his Harley in gear even as eggs were popping all around him, U-turning in a tire-screaming rage and speeding on a direct line to where my feet were scratching for traction he caught me skating on weak ankles. *Oh, shit!* I thought as the motorcycle closed in behind a piercing light. I wasted a precious second deciding that running directly at him to get by wouldn't work; he had closed the angle too much for me to get by and I just knew he would have used his bike to stop me.

Cripes, what would my father do if the cops brought me home for this, for throwing eggs at a police officer for God's sake? The mayor, the police, the whole city knew who my father was and they respected his integrity.

I was running with all my might, scanning desperately for a fence hole to zip through. The alley lit up like prison searchlights and the motorcycle's roar got bigger. I heard the thing skidding to a stop behind me, sensed the dust cloud its tires kicked up just as I spotted an open back gate and veered sharply through. Suddenly hitting damp grass my feet shot out from under me and I hit the ground on an angle. Fast as I could I popped up, knowing another missed beat would put me in deep jeopardy. I could feel the police officer's presence and my mind flashed the image of a fire-snorting bull thumping across the grass. I was too panicked to register where an escape gate might be and I didn't have time anyway. That police officer had beaten me in every facet of our game and I was gripped by the absolute fear that comes from having to face a man who was that enraged.

WUUUUNNNNNNNGGGGG!

History would note that one slightly sagging clothesline caught one hard-charging Windsor Police officer across the chest at precisely that blink in time. And that one black-booted foot kicked rapidly skyward at the same time the rear knee buckled, tilting a flailing form rapidly backwards. The whole thing crashed hard with the ground and didn't even bounce. Air fled his lungs in a *huhhh!* and he went limp.

I was gone. Over the fence in a flash and flying through the adjoining yard. I took a route home through alleys and along the dark edges of streets, moving with stealth at an extraordinary rate of speed.

I fretted for days like only a frightened fourteen-year-old can, sneaking looks at the newspaper to see if any cops had been reported hurt while chasing "unknown assailants." It was a good while before my paranoia would calm and I promised God I'd never fool around with the cops again, not that way anyway. When I told Paul about retiring from that activity he merely chuckled and found another to partner with.

Our original group of two had by then expanded. Earl Assarica had joined Paul and I, followed by others until the gang sometimes numbered as many as seven, all with strong throwing arms and some with legendary throwing arms.

Earl was slight and fragile-appearing. I thought his family situation was dreadful. With a father defeated by a serious alcohol affliction while his mother's light slowly dimmed from the effects of dis-ease we sensed but couldn't define Earl saw life from a different viewpoint.

Earl was our friend and until mainstream Canadians disdained him we didn't see where his life understanding differed from ours; we were from the same planet, we ran the same streets and knew the same secret hiding places. And like Earl, who received a more potent allocation, we sensed the rejection, picking up a subtle feeling we were unable to translate into thoughts during our excursions away from home surroundings, forays that evolved into nighttime sneak-and-snatch operations into the kitchens of central Windsor restaurants.

Those operations got their beginning one half-moon night as Earl, Paul and I strolled down the middle of a downtown alley during a casual routine outing. The kind of aromas that create dampness on the walls of a meat-eater's mouth halted us directly under an elevated window where someone had placed a platter of just sizzled steaks. Earl's nose perked and within seconds I, being taller than Paul, was tottering on Earl's shaky shoulders, reaching overhead to snatch and then drop the steaks to Paul, who couldn't handle the heat. It didn't occur to me to take the whole platter. So Paul fumbled with the steaks below whispering, *"Ow! Shit! Damn!"* Earl, barely able to support my weight and worried sick that someone dangerous to the operation could be alerted, was most emphatic in urging me to "Hurry *up*, you fuck head!"

Though impregnated with alley grit the steaks were an absolute treat and three ravenous outcasts attacked them with savage pleasure. That one event was so gratifying we decided to expand the service to select other places of fine downtown dining.

Restaurant people became acutely aware of our threat to their inventory without actually knowing whom they were contending with. It must have been a little disorienting to set a pot down, leave it long enough to check something else and seconds later be wondering where your roast of dead cow had gone.

Efforts to resolve their dilemma made careful planning

essential if we were to continue securing food that attended to various hungers—that of adventure for some and for others nourishment of a type that was otherwise unavailable. The operations became riskier and at times group-members narrowly survived incidents when getting caught was as tight as breaking free of someone's grasp and fleeing. Or being in full flight, straining mightily to make it past the back door ambush awaiting pursuers, for the escape route was usually covered by guys who could cut loose with a withering barrage of stones, eggs and old fruit.

One restaurant crew designed a trap that our group's advance scout identified. Walking down a familiar alley he noticed that a rear door floodlight that should have been on wasn't on so he drifted into some shadows to pee.

"Psst…"

The advance guy pretended not to hear.

"Psssstt!"

No response.

"Hey kid…" in an aggravated whisper.

"Who's there?" in an exaggerated reaction.

"*Quiet!* Not so loud, kid."

"I can't see you. Why you hidin' back there?"

"Never mind, just go away, kid."

"What?"

"Go a-*way!*"

"Why?"

"Beat it or I'll bust your ass."

"What?"

"Beat it, you little asshole, or I'll crack your ribs!"

"Okay, okay, but I gotta pee first. Why're you hidin' back there in the dark?"

"Never mind that, Shithead, just clear your little ass out!"

Laughing, he reported that they were armed with mop handles and probably an overkill of throwing items. They were also bunched to spring from a narrow walkway that was perfect for raining rocks on them from both ends. The raiding party debated briefly whether to ambush their ambush and establish whom they were messin' with but decided to strike that restaurant off our yummy list and visit retaliation on them at a more favorable time. A couple of us voted to put it on them while we had this gift of an opportunity but the majority seemed to think that kind of action would create a war-like relationship it was best to avoid. Being outsmarted and handed a serious whipping in the deal was guaranteed to prime them. Heck, the effect of stealing their food upset them enough. Raising lumps on their heads took it too far.

Johnny Patterson was so strong on retaliating that he wouldn't wait, hurling a red clay brick into the kitchen's giant exhaust fan a few nights later. The impact that brick made with those whirling blades was spectacular. Panicked patrons and employees, thinking explosion, emptied out through front and rear doors like potatoes tumbling out of a burlap sack.

On our next safari through that territory we noticed that thick steel bars had been secured in place to shield the fan. The back door was never again accessible and a powerful, mesh-protected light flooded a newly created zero zone.

Until reaching the age of sixteen we weren't concerned with legal punishment; the law itself was a toothless old tabby we pretended to be scared by. The Caucasian men who administered their law had no clue who we were and substituted authority in place of respect, activating in us the rumblings of rebellion. A couple of us took gleeful advantage of the few opportunities we received to throw rocks in the summer and winter snowballs at the person's car who presided over Juvenile Court, an English gentleman we were obliged to humbly address as "Mr. Burt."

This bunch represented only a small cell of risk-takers relative to the overall community population and ain't that how it is in life? Most McDougall Street kids stayed close to the neighborhood or they didn't possess a feeling for adventure that energized the lower McDougall Street group I was part of. They would, however, participate in other activities, particularly during the summer when a flight of neighborhood doves spread their sexual wings.

Eunice Pettiford was a single, working mother who departed her Mercer Street bungalow at pretty much the same time every workday morning, leaving her two teenagers, Mary Ann and Doody, pretty much on their independent own. Both blossomed that summer, Mary Ann heterosexually, Doody the other way. Several others caught the scent and word spread like lava down a lush mountainside, summoning others who were responding to the same inner messages.

We already possessed a voyeur's interest from peeping into bedrooms, sneaking up on cars rocking in the moonlight and maybe even peeking in on Mom and Dad when they were swept away in that zone.

The beginning group consisted of Mary Ann, Doody and a few secretive others who tried keeping the treasure of pleasure a private matter, but something so new, so exciting, something so *forbidden*, something we had whispered about was actually happening in our here and now. The biggest turn-on for some of the guys was the realization of finally being able to take a girl's panties off and the girl actually *wanting* a guy to do it.

The morning sun saw bushes, an abandoned car, any out of eyesight spaces become hiding places where crotch-hot kids waited for Mrs. Pettiford to leave for work. When she did we descended on her house like dogs chasing spring. Pulled down shades transformed the house and we "did it" in jam-session rotation. And, as was the case in our outdoor activities, rookie flubs became timeless dubs, like the voice of one frustrated friend lamenting in a dark bedroom, "I can't find the hole."

Summer ended and we reluctantly returned to school. This during an era when the British flag—the Union Jack—flew from Canadian flagpoles and school children were programmed with British dogma administered mostly by pink-skinned board-backs with inwardly puckered assholes. We called them "Sir," and it wasn't out of the ordinary for some of these unapproachable classroom monarchs to abuse pupils. That they did so with impunity seemed to me to be part of their teaching mandate. One grade eight teacher, for example, a wordless wretch with pig jowls that sagged his face, was well known for his willingness to thump the back of a head with his hard cover text book, the man's substitute erection. Add to the equation an art teacher whose anger we were at the naked mercy of. This man had a bent for erupting into sudden maniacal rages and once the guy, who may have been in his thirties, grabbed Earl by the nape of his neck and hurled the kid forehead-first into the art room door. This in retaliation for Earl's reflexive "Ugh" to the teacher's repugnant art. The manual arts instructor got his jollies by beating the flesh of a boy's palms with the flat of a steel ruler. It seemed he saw this as a test of wills. The instructor would lay that steel across a palm with a smack that screamed pain until the kid cried or until his hands were so puffed and hurt he couldn't use them. This happened to me. I refused to give him the satisfaction of seeing me cry, finally feeling the tears build, fleeing his class and pedaling home on my bike, steering with my forearms and crying. (Although my father complained to the school principal the teacher was shielded by that same disgusting code criminals, lawyers and cops use to cover their butts when they've wronged.) Lastly, include in that group a female who possessed a face that would have been lovelier than lilacs were it not for an inner ugliness that rendered her hard-featured and mannish. Because this beast that posed as a school-teacher was so intimidating I literally dumped in my pants and sat in the stink rather than persist after she denied my request to be excused. This woman's passion shot to pleasure heaven when she strapped youngsters in a love-what-I'm-doing/hate-who-I'm-doing-it-to performance. She was so intense in punishing us that she'd raise up off both heels to get maximum leverage, puffing up in the cheeks and bringing her strap down with all the snort she could put into it. One time Earl, who seemed to exist in dis-favor, snatched his hand back at just about mid stroke, causing the woman to deliver a resounding whack to her own thick thigh. The sound that fled that beast's lungs hit like a coyote in a cave, reverberating through hallways with an effect that caused doors that were closed to fly open and open doors to snap shut.

These people were sources for us to learn fear, contempt and hatred. Their pomposity, cruelty and bigotry contributed directly to marginalizing us and to the ultimate waste of many good souls. Resenting some of our teachers required zero effort and learning from them was an assignment that never completed. Some children withdraw, other children shrink from adults who would exploit their vulnerability and all kids possess a sense of who's real and who's role-playing.

For many of us the time we spent in those 1940s and 1950s classrooms was charged with fear and chilled by uncertainty. I felt that as a McDougall Street youngster I couldn't possibly know what to expect. Compounding the injustice, these children were deemed incorrigible and unteachable malcontents by the very people who abused them, causing the system to push them deeper into You Don't Belong. The effects of that kind of disrespect carry into adult life, translating into a devaluing that affects the victim like a cancer that attacks their reason for living until they finally die, having spent their lives in shadows. *Why have I been punished for what you have done to me?* Or they seethe, consumed by resentment and inner rage, venting on loved ones without the slightest notion why. Others might take flight, to become restless spirits who spend their lives seeking a place of welcome. Very few accept the experience as part of their process and move on. Everyone would be happier without it.

School days commenced with standard Christian prayers, followed by the singing of "God Save the King," a humorless-looking criminal in military garb whose grey-toned portrait hung in a place of honor across from the principal's office. Our studies connected to the British Empire and colonized Canadians sang to British glory, nonsense like "Ruuulle Brit-tann-iaaa, Britannia rule the waves, Brit-ons never, never, *nev*-errrrr shall be slaves…" without being informed that Britain had enslaved most of the planet, that the English routinely violated defenseless nations, that Canada was merely another British "possession." No one mentioned that the Canada we sang about was a materialist's dream, a prized acquisition consisting of exploitable resources and vast land holdings that had previously been inhabited by a noble and trusting people who had been horribly treated. There was no portrayal of these original inhabitants as being put upon by uninvited English "settlers," ruthless primitives who arrived with bibles, guns, greedy intentions, the British flag and disease. And when little Canadian children stood at military attention in their classrooms and sang "God save our grac-ious king, long live our noh-ble king, God save the kinngggg..." no one dared tell them that the crown worn by George the noble British king had passed along a line of lunatics who murdered their wives, ordered people's death and dispatched the mighty British military to commit global crime in servitude to the British hierarchy.

Then one day George VI, King of England and ruler of an empire on which, they boasted, "the sun never set," died of cancer, having lived few days without masses of murdered people in his portfolio. In passing on to wherever people like him go he made way for his daughter to seat herself on England's gilded throne and traditionalists the world over were thereafter obligated to waste a portion of their day in the same singsong praise of yet another royal parasite, this one female.

Under those terms school was, at best, a difficult experience. Not once, not for one day during my tenure in the learning institution did I feel that my personhood was respected. Looking back I can count on the fingers of one hand the teachers (Arthur D. Kidd, Mrs. Katz, Eddie Dawson and Dorothy Taylor—thank you) whom I felt valued me as a meaningful human being. I felt little reason to become involved in an institution where it was compulsory to sit (or be punished) and try to keep your mind from going to more stimulating places while the world's dullest mouths anesthetized one's incentive to be present. We were offered no alternatives, accorded no choice nor solicited for even a smidgen of input. There was absolutely nothing, *nada*, not so much as a minute that resembled the concept of "Hey kid, tell us what you think, how you feel, what you'd appreciate from us in our responsibility to you." Speaking your mind could get you shamed, hurt, cast out or treated like you didn't matter. Time in the learning institution came on with repetitions of *Do this or else*. That approach—"Do this or I'll hurt you, humiliate you, take away your freedom, confiscate your personal property"—has been a preferred method of persuasion for so long that folks believe it's normal business. They seem to believe it's the way life *is* because using power over each other is how we've traditionally carried on. *Do this or else!* is the classroom monarch method of intimidation, not teaching, the way some parents manage their children and how most religions keep their herds rounded up. For me and for many of my *compadres* "Do this or else" generated a resentful "Fuck yourself" feeling and kids who feel that way rarely move on to higher forms of formal education. I could barely wait for the ending-day bell to relieve my confinement in that uncomfortable place. Every day I watched for the clock to crawl to that spot where I could finally release to be secure among other spirits who were wild and free, just like me.

An unforgiving Christian god was strong on McDougall Street, making an appearance every Sunday at the British Methodist Episcopal Church and my child's mind surmised it was probably the same god we beseeched to save the British sovereign.

There were certain ways we were expected to regard God, like being required to spell His name starting with a capital letter.

God…whose son Jesus was presented in the form of a benevolent Caucasian man. How does that imagery work in a kid's little mind? If God's son is a Caucasian male it makes logical sense that God must be a Caucasian male, would you agree? So if Mom and Dad push little Open Mind into revering Jesus does it install the unconscious understanding that Caucasian men are godlike? Where does that scenario position everyone who *isn't* a Caucasian male?

From early in life we were given to believe we wanted God to take us to a spot that religion administrators promoted as a better place God had set aside exclusively for dead Christians. Lots of folks heard about Heaven but no one I knew ever actually *saw* Heaven. Lots of folks bought the illusion without thinking about the blatant discrimination that's part and parcel of Reserved for Christians Only. Also during that period in our lives parents encouraged their little godlets to recite this little ditty: "Now I lay me down to sleep, I pray the Lord my soul to keep. If I should die before I wake, I pray the Lord my soul to take." I usually added a few special requests, like asking God to look out for our dog Pal and other cherished beings, like Uncle Albert and Aunt Rosie Timbers. Then I crawled between clean sheets but sometimes I couldn't sleep because the fear of dying while I slept was deep in my mind. I didn't really want to go to Heaven anyway. I was content to live on McDougall Street and Heaven was someone else's idea. On the other hand, trying to reach sleep without paying respects to God was a risk because He might see that you didn't wake up.

Do this or else, little boy.

Households of that period didn't have televisions blinking back from Living Room Central and personal computers hadn't been conceived so neighborhood kids didn't laze around indulging in the fat-munchies, choosing instead to venture into an expanding universe. Or we played high-pitched scrub softball in a vacant lot every summer day and in the winter we played nostril-flaring ice hockey on the frozen rinks of Wigle Park. On any given day we could assemble a number of the city's finest natural athletes, summoning one another through a communication system that saw kids awaken with the same feeling about what and where.

Forty-five years after I have moved away from the old neighborhood my kids, who have never visited McDougall Street, could go there on their own and after introducing themselves be embraced like a returning son by those who have survived.

To think that I felt shame at being raised on McDougall Street. The familiarity. The honesty. Mentoring from our older generations. Our closeness. Unforgettable life experiences we shared. Timeless acceptance of one another. The love that sees me stay in touch with community elders. That was how our community was and how it is with us.

Now to the experiences of an alien son in mainstream Canada.

Where Are You From?

When Moe Sihota was the British Columbia Minister Responsible for Multiculturalism & Immigration I attended a holiday gathering in his ministerial office. It was a surprisingly informal celebration in an official setting, due essentially to Mr. Sihota's casual nature.

While circulating the way people do at those functions I felt myself being tracked by a woman I wasn't motivated to meet at the time. There's something we sense about peoples' motives, you know? Disregarding a pretty clear message she walked up to me with an engaging smile and said, "My what an exotic looking man you are," followed by, "where are you from?" It was an innocent question that didn't offend, although I have a full life of experience contending with a mentality that insists people who look like me are alien within Canadian culture. As this attitude persists there've been manifest in some instances a childlike curiosity, in others a sincere wish to learn more about someone who is "different" and at times a stance that states, "You are not like us and we don't accept you." All express the belief that I am alien. To the curious woman who regarded me as "exotic" I responded gently, "I'm from Canada, madam," followed by, "Welcome to my country."

If you think someone is different from you, please consider for a minute that you're also different and it's really not necessary to do anything out of the ordinary about being different. It's not necessary to discuss being different and it's not necessary to celebrate your differences. Billy William Pritchard? Did you say that we need do nothing more than quietly accept who we are?

Province of British Columbia grants are used to fund many agencies that serve the immigrant community providing language lessons, coaching in job search techniques and providing access to other transition services that enable newcomers to assimilate into the mainstream Canadian lifestyle. To qualify for B.C. government funding there are guidelines that must be adhered to—controls, basically.

When I worked as a contract consultant for one of the funding provincial ministries a high-salaried decision-maker told me that she refused to fund African groups "because they don't know what to do with the money." Yes she did. She looked me straight in the face and made the statement with complete and arrogant conviction. The woman added that she deliberately withheld funding from a Vancouver organization that served the immigrant community because she "personally didn't like" the outspoken Committee for Racial Justice director, a crusader for fairness named Aziz Khaki.

In my television documentary *Racism in Victoria, A Silent Tragedy*, Dr. Joseph Schaeffer, an evolved soul who prefers being just plain Joe, cited the example of a young New Canadian from Central America by way of the United States. This young lady stated that she "liked it a lot better in the United States because there people knew they were racist whereas in Canada it's a much bigger problem, particularly in the school she found herself in, because as she put it, 'Nobody here thinks they are.'"

Prisoners Of Mother England?

In 1994 this writer interviewed to fill a management position in the boxing venue during the Victoria Commonwealth Games (formerly the British Empire Games). This was a full-time volunteer position with a three-interview screening process. An ex IBMer, I put on my best conservative front, updated my resume, dusted off my reference letters and submitted to the interview process. The first was with a woman who scrutinized my employment history. The second was with a male who also examined my work experience and asked about my boxing background. Each interview lasted the better part of a structured hour. The third, in the same spacious conference room, involved the original woman and man from interviews one and two and sitting at the far end of the conference table was a new face. This figure, a retired school principal, was clearly the Head Man In Charge (HMIC).

"Why," I asked, "are you sitting way down at that end of the table?" which may have been twenty or so feet away. If I had taken the offered seat I and HMIC's two lieutenants would be separated from him by distance that confirmed a status I couldn't see any need to validate. The gentleman replied that he was more at ease in that position, the effect of which neutralized when I declined the chair that placed me at the opposite end crosshaired between his subordinates. These two silently joined after I took a seat to his immediate right.

Their questions were tedious, having to do with how was I qualified to fill the position and why should they allow me to fill it?

"Hey, hang tight for a minute," I said after a while, holding my hand up to slow the flow. "I need to understand something. Is this a full-time, non-paid volunteer position we're talking about?"

"Why, yes it is."

"Okay, let's check this from another perspective. You guys've been asking what qualifications I bring to the position," and the unspoken message was, "like you're doing me a favor." A person should get at least a facsimile of balance and being given to believe I was being graced with the privilege to work long hours for no pay presented too much tilt. "You've asked about my contribution to you and now I need you to tell me what I can expect *from* you."

All three fell silent, looking mechanically from one to another and then the two secondary people turned to the HMIC. Looking most officious, almost military in his bearing he said, "You'll have an opportunity to host the Queen."

I wish I could remember if there was a "harrumph" or two in there.

Having any kind of contact with this person doesn't qualify as an honor in my book. To me the woman represents generations of crooked dealings, theft, unjust incarceration, murder and genocide against people I'm descended from—African, Indian and Scottish.

Extinct is a chain reaction that begins with the first insane killing.

Whoa, whoops, hold on, partner. "Hosting the British Queen is hardly an honor," I responded. "However, if you can visualize my shaking her hand, introducing myself on a first-name basis and regarding her on equal terms we might move on to the next stage in this process. But I think it's best for me to withdraw, would you agree?"

By Jove, Regis, *did* they. And when I took leave of their silence it was with the feeling they thought the applicant had declined a rare opportunity.

Ultimately I became one of three boxing venue Media Relations Officers for those 1994 Commonwealth Games (referred by some attendees as the "Colonial Games"). During this posting I managed to expose to African nations that the British were cheating, something that was entirely unnecessary; it appeared to me that Britain was being favored in the rendering of decisions anyway. Even with this, members of the British team were slipping up to the television broadcast booth to sneak a peek at monitors that displayed the judges' scoring between rounds. Relaying that information to their boxer before the next round got underway provided the edge that comes from knowing. Coupled with the favorable decisions, this additional dishonesty prompted a meeting of African team officials who threatened to walk out.

Later I realized I placed greater faith in directly passing the information along than in trusting boxing officials—the Old Boys Club—to take action against Mum's brave lads.

.

Somehow we're given to believe that because something has always been a certain way that it should always be that same certain way.

Commonality

The South African apartheid system got its parentage from the same strategy practiced by the invader to control inhabitants of the possession that was called Canada. In that their goal is to keep people separate and under control there's a connecting line between a South African "township" and a Canadian Indian "reserve."

Above the entrance to Indian reservations could be posted in bold English script: "We Will Keep you Poor, Controlled, Disempowered, Degraded, Distressed, Depressed and Ours To Do With As We Will. God Save the Queen."

Every now and then I play friendly 8-Ball with a present day Canadian male who was so proud of his accomplishment in being chosen to be part of a government land/ treaty negotiating team that he couldn't see past his personal agenda. I asked, "How can you possibly negotiate to 'give' self governing privileges to people your ancestors ruthlessly took away from them? How can you negotiate to allocate and then divvy-up land with descendants from whose people your ancestors stole the land? Because you have control of it doesn't make the land yours and you have no rights of negotiation for stolen property. If anything, the government you serve in this charade should be paying reparations and apologizing most humbly." This flesh and blood tool for the system will, however, play with commitment but without conscience the role he feels honored to fill, having expressed the feeling that, "someone has to fuck these people."

The Imperialist is still with us.

Why are addiction, abuse, suicide, murder and incarceration disproportionate among native spirits who were once at peace within and in harmony with their universe? From the movie *Thunderheart:* "Let's face it, you're a conquered people."

I think that if I were to choose suicide—and thoughts about suicide have occasionally invaded the corners of my stability—I would make that choice because I preferred the finality of death to the prospect of another empty day of life in chains.

In some countries the oppressor hunts native people down and kills them. In others the oppressor herds them into a place of control where the process of spiritual death begins their ending. Assassinate the spirit and it will most assuredly follow that you have killed the mind and the body as well.

A wise man from my youth once said, with reference to Nazi atrocities against Jewish people, "At least they were open and honest."

Have you seen any of the graduates of Canada's Indian Residential Schools who wander a fogged wilderness, awaiting Death after having their lives impounded at birth? Victimized by the Crown and marginalized by the Country. Yes, *those* people. The term "Canada's Indians" consciously describes their place; these dehumanized beings were regarded as chattels of the British Crown. As such they were robbed of their heritage and raped of their human rights.

Could it be, do you think, Gary, that achieving fairness in Canada requests involvement by an international judiciary armed with a genuine, politics-free commitment to ensuring wrongs made right? Since achieving fairness hasn't been achieved, isn't being achieved and doesn't look like it's in any danger of being achieved in the near future, the answer begs.

Is help on the horizon?

At no time in history have a conqueror's motives been philanthropic.

If you should encounter an elderly native Indian with scars that look like punctures healed over the top and under the bottom lips, try to visualize having your lips sewed together as punishment for speaking your native tongue.

At the time, which mighta been ten years after WWII, I laughed when my pal Leonard Flatley eased up behind high school classmate Otto Schlappner and hissed "*Nat-zee*" into Otto's ear. There was everything German about Otto and nothing Nazi about Otto but Otto was German and the Nazi movement had been a German tragedy.

Someone tole me that after he left the nest Len became an advocate of Canadian Indian rights and died, it was said after he fell off the back of a truck in British Columbia. I was tole that he married an Indian woman but I don't really know and maybe I shouldn't be repeating hearsay. The last time I saw him, we did some herb in inner city Detroit and there were little brown kids hanging all over him like he was Oak Tree and calling his name with a feeling that comes from a heart that's been freed to trust. I don't know what ever became of Otto but I would sure like to know.

The other day I saw two North American Indians in a Royal Canadian Mounted Police cruiser. One of these traitors to Indian history was driving and the other was riding shotgun. You must be unaware, young warriors, that Robin Hood is a myth and that the specter of the Sheriff of Nottingham feeds on the Canadian psyche. Have you not been attentive to recent Indian history, to continuing Indian history? Next time your blood people protest another injustice and this force you've joined is turned against them consider that the red tunic you violate your heritage with is stained with a history of Indian blood.

Although you shouldn't be in a position of *having* to aspire, if you *do* aspire to secure just practices for your people, if you possess the strength needed to work for change from within what you know to be a force that practices racism and can do so without oppressing your brothers or compromising your self there's a place in the Accomplishment Hall of Fame waiting for you. Keep in mind always that the oppressor traditionally conscripts compromised spirits to bear his arms in suppression of their own people. Be aware also that the master creates illusions about these turncoats, fabricating them into heroes who faithfully serve the motherland—and that's a key, that they *serve*, and have you seen any fabricated into commanding positions? Think, Red Coat Enforcer of the Queen's law…in your whole life have you ever seen an illustration of *any* kind depicting a handful of horse-mounted brown officers commanding masses of pink foot soldiers?

Sometimes you can see what it *is* by recognizing what *isn't*, eh what Magee?

Coming truly together creates its own place.

In the summer of 1998 my fifteen-year-old and two pals were strolling through James Bay, a section that's a few steps up the social ladder from the Victoria West district where he lived with his mother, when Victoria City Police accosted them. The kid was attired in a standard of the day's teenager, which included a backpack he keeps his graffiti pens in. Yep, he's a graffiti artist, passionately drawn in to this form of expression. He's taken me to see complete walls where this unique craft is practiced. The artwork's amazing. He uses a fairly decent Japanese camera to record these constantly changing expressions and the kid's put together a collection of some good art. But let's get back to their encounter with police authorities. His story to me was that a male and a female stopped them, searched them, went through their backpacks and confiscated their graffiti pens, one of which had set Beau back twelve bucks. As he talked about the situation I was impacted by his acceptance. It was not unusual, he indicated, for police to violate what would be inviolable human rights in a more progressive setting. No, he didn't like it but what could he do?

I telephoned police headquarters and made an appointment to meet with the appropriate officers, who were gracious in a rigid way. My first question addressed whether a crime had been committed, if anyone had seen the boys defacing private property. No, the police officers hadn't actually seen either boy with a marking instrument in his hand but there was recent graffiti in the vicinity. The next question had to do with the absence of grounds for stopping them, searching them and in effect stealing their personal property. Police officers required only the suspicion that a crime had been committed, I was told. Suppose the kids refused to co-operate, I asked. Resisting a police officer will get you placed under arrest. (This reminded me of the twenty-eight year old immigrant Ethiopian who told me he had been asked by the bouncer in a popular Yates Street drinking establishment to step outside which he did, leaving his drink, change, cigarettes and a blue-eyed woman. Once outside the bouncer bullied the slightly built young man and signaled two uniformed constables who were sitting in a police cruiser at the curb. The African was forced front-down on the sidewalk while his hands were shackled behind him preparatory to a paddy wagon trip to the lock-up. Once there he was made to strip to his shorts, placed in a jail cell and released next morning without explanation, but with a warning that he was lucky to not be charged with resisting arrest).

"With this as your mandate, do you wonder why kids don't respect you?" I asked.

Being respected was secondary to enforcing the law.

"Even when your enforcement practices violate a human's rights?"

"We don't view the doing of our job as violating rights."

And the justification for taking their personal property? If kids followed your example, if they took something from another person the same way they had their property taken away by you they would be put through some changes for theft.

"When we think a crime is being committed we're allowed to confiscate instruments of that crime."

We may as well have been in Gestapo Headquarters. Except for this effort to bring into the light the oppressive and culturally ignorant ways of some darned people there was little else I could do other than suggest providing a place where kids could just go and splash to their heart's satisfaction. Imagine the conflict that would die when two opposing forces resolved that no amount of rules or punishment can stop artists from expressing themselves. Give an artist a place to freely exercise their passion and that artist will cease defacing your mailboxes.

The suggestion notwithstanding, we successfully requested the return of their property and we were also able to leave police headquarters without being jailed for resisting arrest.

People don't resist, resent or rebel without just cause.

Flying Barbara told about a controlling person who asked their lover, "Are you rebelling?" Really. *Are you rebelling?* That one adult in an intimate relationship with another would even *think* they could set in a place the other person would need to rebel against is an insult and an outrage. Even so, Flying Barbara said, suppose the question had been, "Are you rebelling against my controlling ways?" thereby opening two doors to the same place. "Why, yes I am. Whaddaya wanna do about it?" When folks acknowledge that, "You do this in relationship to my doing that," don't they create a place to start from, something to work with, the shared solving of which could move them closer together? Otherwise, I'll concentrate on your reaction to my stuff, never look at my responsibility in our difficulty and we go nowhere together.

Whether it's a clenched-up little two-year old rebelling against parental dominance or sullen teens struggling against forced anything or entire populations in revolt against oppressive regimes, people seem to experience the same process: Resistance, Resentment, Rebellion and Revolt, always, though not exclusively in reaction to repression, oppression and control.

Do you wonder why it is that one specific group—Caucasian men—control *all* significant power places in Canadian society? I sure do. I know already that if all the cards are under the control of one person the card game's loaded in that person's favor. I need to understand how that person got control of the cards and why this game we're caught up in should keep on playing by the same old rules.

Do I Have To Give Up Me
To Be Employed By You?

Bad Jesse knew a woman who was so hunched by fear that she was incapable of expressing her indignity to male colleagues who had displaced the lady from her office, stuffing her belongings in boxes on the floor and saying nary a word about it. So she walks into her office and *blam!* the effect of their deed smacks her like a bag of ice in the face. To challenge the power of these boys by confronting their arrogance would have generated consequences—*Shreeeek. Screee…What will these guys do to me if I tell them how I feel about what they did to me?*—she was so terrified of risking that she fled into an oft-used role of victim. Po' me. BJ added that at some earlier time in life she had moved into collecting photo memories and "things" that she manipulated to create impressions she could peek from behind. Now she takes prescription drugs to cope and she wonders that she's still disabled from connecting with who she is.

At various times older conservative African Canadian men would ask, "What will the white man think if you don't behave the way you're supposed to?" I can't guess how many times I heard that acknowledgement but I know exactly how many concurred when the response was, "He'll think whatever he chooses and what he thinks has absolutely nothing to do with me."

If you don't grant authority over you to another they can't exercise authority over you. No matter what it may be, without your consent it can't happen.

An observation posed as a question, John R: Is it said (and if so how widely do you think?) that Canadians have traded—sacrificed—their freedom for security?

Mutual Victims

When I lived in Victoria the coppers routinely installed at various strategic points late-night roadblocks they called drunk driving "Counter Attacks." In this practice there's an absence of respect for the rights of non-drinking drivers who necessarily wait in line to be asked, "Have you had anything to drink?" and maybe, "Where have you been tonight?" Such a crappy position to put a cop in, stopping people on their way home at night and asking them questions like that.

Not playing the game can get you pulled over, where authority wrinkles into a different face. And don't even *think* about responding with, "Where I've been is really none of your business, constable." Or if you want to enhance the chance of getting your head busted, "Hey, baby, that ain't none yo' bidnez." Occasionally however, there's a "Gee, I'm sorry. I know it's a problem for you and I hope you understand." That in order to catch a few you must inconvenience many? I appreciate your courtesy but I still don't understand and I don't accept when weighing the effects of that use of authority. I see police officers and motorists alike as victims of this way of doing business, which doesn't appear to bring them closer together.

It's enough to drive a guy to drink, hey Chuckles?

It's about eight o'clock on a mild March night and I'm depleted after working a long, strenuous Saturday for my favorite bank employer. My senses are so dimmed they don't register a wrong way turn into a one-way street but they're brought up by the sudden light show atop a Portland police cruiser directly across the street. I pull over to the curb wondering what I did wrong, my old blue station wagon bathed in red, blue and bright spot light as the cruiser pulls in behind. I get out of my car, the police officer comes out of the lights saying, "Hey partner, I bet you didn't know you just turned the wrong way into a one-way street."

"Aw shucks," I respond, "I thought I was at Martin Luther King, Junior Boulevard." There's minimal traffic on this Northeast Portland night; no car drives past and I notice the headlights of only one, which turns right a half dozen or so blocks away.

"You're off by a couple of blocks," the officer informs. "You got B.C. plates on your car, what're you doin' here?" he asks, more out of curiosity. A man I judged to be in his late twenties, his jacket is open, no hat on his head, he has a goatee and a smile lightens everything about him.

I show him University of Portland brochures and explain that

I'm establishing a homestead in preparation to my college-age son moving to Portland.

The officer is warm and comforting, "Great. Welcome to Oregon," he says. "Suppose you pull a U-turn to get you back on track and I'll cover you from behind," which he did, turning in a perfectly synchronized U with lights still flashing. I hooked right at the corner, noticing his lights extinguish as he broke off, having completed a transaction with someone whose respect he had just exercised the freedom to win.

To Judge And To Judge

Last I heard British Columbia judges, those people charged with the duty of administering law, are employed by the Ministry of the Attorney General. With this way of doing business the judiciary gets to operate like a private club, a closed society of untouchables who exercise incredible power over citizens they're purportedly in office to serve. Something wrong with that picture, Edward. Sit yourself quietly in a Canadian courtroom sometime if you'd care to witness the actions of someone outfitted with black robes who's been empowered to pretend God. Not that all judges are power-based so much as the law itself is based in power that can severely affect someone's life. Would you say that appearing in a Canadian courtroom can be terrifying, Suitcase? Would you say also, Suitcase, that the law isn't a tool for authoritarian rule? That the law is an instrument for fairness, that law enforcement people aren't in place to oppress and they have no right to act like terrorists?

I feel that I have the right to be judged with respect and treated as a person. Regardless of whether I come under a judge's power as a minor traffic offender or as a serious criminal I'm entitled to be treated like a person. And I think a way for that to happen requests a democratic something like the vote. Time's ripe, overdue actually, for folks to decide the kind of law person who qualifies to judge them. For God's sake, Canada, these people are supposed to be *civil servants*. Their responsibility is to you, to serve your needs and you people *are their employer*. Democratically speaking, you have the right to judge who these people should be and your vote can decide whether they *should* be judging you. Shucks, Arthur Marvin, sometimes it ain't just streets that need cleaning up.

Democratically speaking, that is.

If we don't work our difficulties out, if we don't advance beyond the colonial process our problems will simply continue to hurt.

The Receiver And The Sender

None of us was immune to the sender of racism role. We were bloody-well racist in our own bloody way, treating newly arrived bloody Italians in the most unwelcome fookin' manner.

It stands to reason that if you're raised in a racist environment that you'll be programmed with racist input. Therefore when considering our mind food of the period it's not surprising that we called these New Canadians names like "New Canadians", "Dagos", "Wops" and we joked about them like they were dirt. Jewish people? Although we didn't call them names some from our group hurled stones through a synagogue window and laughed when a man cautiously cracked open the front door, pleading that a rock had "voonded" someone inside. We acted with the same insensitivity towards Chinese people, marauding through a place called "China Town," harassing shop owners and making light of the way they talked. Once in a while we kicked open wide the door of a drinking establishment owned by a Chinese associate of my father, hollered *"Chink!"* into the place and ran like the dickens. One night the proprietor, a man named Eddie Lee, chased me, ran me down, threw me down and pounced on a screeching, hysterically thrashing kid who didn't think he could be caught. I was terrified, pleading to be released and bawling like *I* was the victim. To this day I believe I was spared grave harm when the man recognized me, for I saw rage that comes from mortal hurt in him.

"Aren't you Ronnie Smith's son?" he asked, his expression transforming to astonishment.

"Yes, Mister, yes I am," I squealed, hoping my father's reputation would help me slither away without being stepped on.

The pain in his face I'll remember forever and I don't want it to be the last vision in my mind when I die. "I don't teach my kids to call you nigger," Mr. Lee said in a voice almost too weak to hear. Releasing me, he rose slowly to his feet and trudged away with his head down.

I haven't seen the gentleman since that night but the message stayed with me. During the process of unlearning my own racism Mr. Lee's words—*I don't teach my kids to call you nigger*—fuel the motivation to cleanse every living cell of the sickness that moved me to demean another person's heritage.

As I recall, some of us Windsor "Negroes" were mindlessly *and* thoughtlessly racist within our own group, feeling poetically accomplished when we regurgitated garbage like "If you're white, you're right. If you're yellow, you're mellow. If you're brown, you can hang around. If you're black, you better get back." We called names like "Kong" and made behind-their-back jokes about darker-browned folks who wore bright colors like red. And because we were so Canadian we also viewed "the dark fellows" as "the dark fellows" and did we snicker at images of them.

That's pretty accomplished stuff, Mum, simultaneously implanting sender *and* receiver roles into one unsuspecting little organism.

It hurt like a dagger into my chest when Gary Goddard said, during a high school pile-up on a fumbled football during a lunchtime game of touch, "There's a nigger in the wood pile." Nobody paid notice but me and prior to now I haven't mentioned the episode, although it passes through my mind every once in while. Of course it wouldn't have had any meaning at all if I hadn't identified with that particular word the way that I did. Gary and I cared for each other like brothers from different orbits and we saw no differences. I haven't seen him in too many years. I'm confident Gary moved on to success within the system. I moved into the place that produced this book and nothing ever came out of that schoolyard woodpile.

My Canadian-born athletic sons don't play ice hockey because playing ice hockey has historically been difficult and unrewarding for folks like us. If you trace the game's North American history you'll see a decidedly Canadian trademark stamped into it—"White man's country, White man's game, keep it that way." (Actually the prejudice originally extended to everyone who wasn't Canadian, especially those damned Americans that Canadians heartily resented.) My sons don't play ice hockey because Canadians who owned the sport abused their father—Windsor Arena rink rats with names like Papazian, Peniche and Sisco routinely made remarks about us "zigaboos" playing organized hockey, saying things like, "They need some 'color' in the league, ha, ha, ha," and beating the snot out of us if we didn't like it. My sons don't play ice hockey because their grandfather died a defeated alcoholic, lamenting his unacceptability by the National Hockey League. A gifted athlete, he felt he coulda been a player but he couldn'ta been a white man and only white men were acceptable in the National Hockey League during his day. Instead he was abused and sometimes humiliated on the minor level and rejected at the major level. There are healthy reasons why my sons don't play ice hockey, which face-off against the unhealthy practices of men who robbed people like their grand-father of his right to play the game. And it's a crime against hockey that in doing so those short-sighted bigots robbed the game and stole from its fans. Who knows how many potential greats were deprived the chance to share gifts that shine for limited time? Bloody good thing Wayne Gretzky wasn't born with skin that narrowed minds retard themselves from relating to, eh Paulywog?

With commercial ice hockey seated securely in an international home and the National Hockey League becoming more an American property it would seem the apartheid barrier is well breached and a process that's creating change is at work. It's a real interesting time in sports and entertainment in general to see how the success of one entity's opening itself up progresses into a success pattern for others to follow. And hey Kirk, it don't matter who gets there first so long as somebody gets to the place where it begins.

Perpetuation

I seem to encounter more Canadians than you can count all day who argue that Canada is *not* a British colony, dammit. People who'll deny seventeen different ways that the effect of a foreign ruler's authority owns a summer cottage in the Canadian mind. An observant person's got to wonder what effect's created when Canadian currency, stamps and the walls of Canadian institutions pay homage to the British throne. Or eyes that take a minute to tally up the provincial ensigns and coats of arms all over Canada that bear the British lion's mark. Cities, streets, rivers, places of honor that constantly imprint British occupation in the mind. Government based on the British system. An obligation to revere British tradition. Why do Canadians bow down like serfs and surrender their integrity to Elizabeth Windsor's presence? In the eyes of folks who peek in from outside the Colonial Circle she's basically a misinformed something in human female form who's got an outdated con working for her, no more, no less. But in places where the British mind rules? She's the Queen of Canada, baby, and her mark is everywhere.

Honestly Russ, you really don't think Canada's a British colony? *And what else would you like to buy sir?*

In all cases it's just a matter of time.

Hey CT, did the stars really blink when Bob Marley said, "Emancipate your mind."?

CT, what do you think would happen if you taught the Marley Philosophy in your London, Ontario public school classroom?

At the time when I received Canadian citizenship in British Columbia on Canada Day 1990 it was part of gotta-do to pledge allegiance to the "Queen of Canada." There was no choice in this—if you wanted Canadian citizenship you had to acknowledge Elizabeth as your queen. Danged if that doesn't place Her higherness than God when you consider that a choice to swear on the Bible or not to swear on the Bible is part of court procedure. Given a choice I would have felt more comfortable honoring the memory of Louis Riel and the courage of every Canadian patriot/ freedom fighter who was outlawed or "executed" according to "law" imposed by servants of the Crown. *Their* law, *our* people. From my point of view a pledge to honor people who lost their lives during the process leading to Canadian independence relates more to the meaning of being Canadian than pledging to an illegitimate authority who symbolizes why those Canadians were put to death.

Consider that the British filched as much of North America as they could get away with and that the southern half of the continent took its independence (freedom) after spanking the British bottom in a determined reaction to imperialism. Northern North America, however, remained a Loyalist stepchild of Mother England, asking to be granted a Bill of Rights that was a birthright southern North America had centuries earlier enshrined. Imagine: "May I please have me rights to be who I am, Mum?" Comparing the growth of both countries a picture assumes form. Kids who get hung up in Mummy's apron strings miss out on entitlement and growth, hey Le Roi?

During the 1968 Russian intrusion into Czech-oslovakia a wise man, responding to my outrage, explained without emotion that the Russians had invaded Czechoslovakia to maintain their balance of economic power. All I had seen was news footage of people under attack by military power and I couldn't get past that. To focus this ageless characteristic of relationship between nations he added, "Be absolutely certain that if Canada—which is merely an economic satellite of the United States—attempted to sever with the United States like the Czechs tried to cut off the Russians an American military force would be patrolling Canadian streets in the blink of an eye."

My mentor didn't mention (because our discussion occurred years before the event) that Canada appears now to be on track to partnership in the United States of North America, a process that looks like it's quietly moving along. The Free Trade Agreement, if you look down the road, just might be a precursor to the United States of North America. Combining American finance and technology with reasonable Mexican labor, plentiful Canadian natural resources and a population conditioned to lay down and roll over before foreign control seems to be a natural. It looks like the Canadian dollar's sliding apathetically into place already.

How is it that people who speak the truth of their minds in repressive places are deemed dangerous and even subversive? Many are ostracized. Some disappear. Or die mysteriously, like from "heart failure." Freedom to speak, however, is freedom to speak regardless. And freedom to be is an undeniable right of birth.

When a United States Marine presented the Canadian flag in an upside-down posture during the 1996 Atlanta Olympic Games, Canadians acted outraged. Could those howls of outrage have been connected to the understanding that an upside-down flag signals a vessel in distress? Could it be that Marine knew what he was doing?

Why do famous Canadians become famous after they've left Canada?

Why does a flower close itself to darkness?

In the early 1970s I enjoyed a marvelous friendship with an almost bilingual female from Lac Saint Jean, Quebec. This refreshingly honest spirit claimed French Canadians were the "nee-gairs of Canada." She believed absolutely that English Canada was obsessed with forcing French Canadians into English Canadian ways, an impossible task; the feeling is that a French Canadian is a French Canadian and you can't expect a French Canadian to regress culturally. If only for this reason if the future runs straight we might see French Canada more vigorously pursue its own destiny, its freedom to be exactly who they are. And why not? *I won't have to battle you in order to be me.* However, the Quebecois effort to assert their cultural rights may witness the Canadian military once more engage in suppression.

Until evolved thinkers engage objectively together in looking into the colonial mind in relationship to these different times things will stay the same. *But...*What would happen if people used divisive issues more as catalysts to bring them together with a shared commitment to working things out?

Lightning invariably strikes the shithouse whenever cultural differences conflict with universal character.

Another Country

At one time I put some thought into developing a poutine specialty restaurant and advertising the product as coming from "Quebec, the Country That Gave Birth to Jean Beliveau," the hockey player who was my childhood hero. I think Quebec also gave birth to Jean Chretien, but how would you know?

In the early Sixties this Ameradian person worked for the IBM Corporation in San Francisco, California and had flown home to Windsor for a short summer visit with my homefolks. While driving along Tecumseh Road I spotted a guy I had played Junior Canadian football with a few years earlier. He looked like he had patterned himself after a silly salesman stereotype, a prematurely paunchy guy wearing a wash 'n' wear short-sleeve shirt, clip-on necktie, wiped off shoes and no-iron britches.

When I pulled my mother's red convertible over and greeted him he wanted to know, "Where do you work?"

"For the IBM Corporation."

"What as," he retorted, "a janitor?"

A popular question asked to the accompaniment of snickers and snorts by some Caucasian males during my younger years was, "Would you want a 'black' man to marry your sister?"

Say, Billy O, why would those gentlemen skirt acknowledging that if she did marry that "black" man their sister would be condemned to the economic deprivation reserved by those Caucasian males for that "black" man?

Really, boys, ya gotta ask yerself too if the "black" man would even want to marry the guy's sister.

My friend Vernon from New Orleans will tell you in a minute that he's no "black" man and Vernon will get righteously literal about it too. Paper is white and ink is black and since Vernon of New Orleans has never seen a human being the color of white paper or of black ink he concludes there are no "black" people and there are no "white" people. As for Vernon, he's American born of African heritage and therefore African American, which connects him to roots that have substance and meaning.

In my personal relationship with Canada at times I clearly see the positives and at times I deeply feel the negatives. In this I am not alone.

You Can Help Me Better
After You Know Me Better

Whilehile working on a contrived television piece that was diverted from its original premise focusing on child abuse to become an appeal for British Columbia provincial government social workers, I observed that social workers appear to be tightly controlled by government policy. It would seem this policy is developed by bureaucrats who are neither from nor of the people whom social workers exercise the awful power of policy over.

Consider that the majority of British Columbia social workers (and judges, police personnel, military personnel, counselors, bureaucrats, etc.), source in a socioeconomic status that stimulates distance from the poor, the deprived and people they see as "different." People like those who aren't tuned in to diverse others are, except in rare cases, disabled from relating in any kind of meaningful way with those "others." To help overcome their inability to relate government workers are required to learn to handle people in a prescribed manner.

What do you imagine would happen if the next graduating social work generation integrated with an older generation of people from "the alien lifestyle" who could guide the young graduates into doing future business and policy shackles went into the recycling bin? Without release from those stifling constraints and respect for the integration of input from my tribe how can I expect anything meaningful from you? Heck Dellygirl, you don't really know who I am and you never will as long as you try to push your ways on me without considering that I have my own ways. How could you possibly know how I feel? I don't think it's being dramatic to ask how can you possibly understand what happens inside me when a Caucasian man who has employment power over me tells racist "jokes" it would be costly to protect myself from. If I challenge him he'll justify a way to get rid of me so that I'm disabled from feeding and housing my family. If the emotional me goes for his throat I end up in jail, yet he has attacked me in the cruelest, most heartless way. He has demeaned my heritage, disrespected me personally and challenged my value, knowing fully that he has the support of a racist system backing him.

Although I hope you're open to acknowledging these conditions I don't expect you to understand the feelings and I hope you never have to go through your days with them.

Where are the people who qualify to understand my life position because they've experienced it? What's more important to my progress in this place, people who read about me or people who know me? *Where are the people like me in this system that attempts to exert authority over me?*

Your system perpetuates the insanity that positions us as intruders. This won't work for my group, it doesn't work for you and no amount of "policy" can make it work for us.

Canada, Canada, Canada . . .

It was a trap that was set up by Canada's elite Airborne Regiment, men whose manhood rites included eating urine-soaked bread and raw human shit. "Rebels" who defiantly flew the American Confederate flag in their barracks, troops who torched the car of a non-commissioned officer who incurred their disfavor.

Using food and water as bait they shot two Somali males in the back after they had taken the bait and were running away. Ahmed Heraho died on the spot. Sixteen year old Shidane Arone wasn't as fortunate; he endured three hours of heinous torture while pleading "Canada, Canada, Canada..." before Death took him. Major Barry Armstrong, a doctor who served in Somalia, alleged that the victim had also been shot in the back of his head execution style at point blank range. Major Armstrong's testimony came in the spring of 1995. The killing had occurred the night of March 4, 1993, a night when the sixteen year old's killers were so moved by their grisly handiwork that they took "trophy" photos of their kill. Imagine, murdering a sixteen-year old boy and then dehumanizing his remains. For men to be so blatant in recording visual images of an act so reprehensible would indicate that the environment was permissive. That they qualified as ignorant in the lowest form is indisputable.

People in power tried to cover the atrocity up—can you imagine? Smoke without fire. Corporal Clayton Matchee, who was supposed to have tried to hang himself in his jail cell with a boot lace was said to suffer brain damage that rendered him "unfit" for trial. Private Kyle Brown was convicted of manslaughter and can you possibly find a way to attach justice to that? Two people shot in the back, one dead, the other wounded, tortured, finally killed with a point-blank bullet into the brain. And premeditated by Canada's elite killing machine, as evidenced by the *setting of a trap.*

Manslaughter? What *does* murder look like?

Two people shot in the back, one dead, the other wounded, tortured, finally killed with a point-blank bullet into the brain and an attitude about responsibility in the country called Canada moves center world stage.

Lieutenant Colonel Carol Mathieu, then commander of the Canadian Airborne Regiment, got the court martial routine. Twice. And found not guilty of dereliction of duty twice. Lieutenant Colonel Mathieu subsequently retired from the military, would you think before a third performance could take stage?

Prime Minister Jean Chretien disbanded the Airborne Regiment, punishing many for the transgressions of a few, dispersing rotten eggs to other baskets in the doing. Bravo, Mr. Prime Minister, yet another stupendous gesture.

Commissioners investigating the affair alleged that senior military officials hiding inside that damned code had altered documents and committed perjury, concluding that without massive change in the military—including a purge of top brass—that things wouldn't get any better.

Government people reacted angrily and ultimately closed the investigation down, confirming once again what Willie John says about Canadians burying their heads in the sand—see nothing, hear nothing and you can see my exposed butt. Defence Minister Art Eggleton rejected the enquiry's report and told reporters, "This happened four years ago. The time for pointing fingers is past." As should be the time for shooting deadly firearms at unarmed young men, Arthur. And how about the time for being responsible for your misdeeds, Mr. Minister? Is that also long past? Does responsibility for performing one's sworn responsibility dissolve after a certain time? How much time would that be, sir? Those two boys are still dead, Arthur. That their lives were torn from them by under-evolved Canadian savages hasn't changed and no amount of time will make it go away. And you're absolutely correct: the time has indeed passed. (The date of these crimes and the subsequent "covering" of it becomes more important with each day that responsibility remains dishonored. What, by the way, is today's date?)

There was talk of the damage this disgrace could cause at the election of that time. After all, it was just two inconsequential "dark fellows" and there were more important matters. Nothing remotely related to justice and honor. Politics and the shading of pink bottoms, folks. Old Boys stuff. Something wrong with that picture too, Boo. And you can be certain that, given similar circumstances, people you have entrusted this lethal power to will do it to you as well and never look back. What's the real story about your guns, by the way?

People who make decisions based on political ambition at the expense of justice prove their inability to justly serve, if service is indeed a function of their office. (Actually, if you think about it, in Canada it seems that the people serve their government more than government employees serve their citizen employers. Hello?).

It would be difficult to cast a vote of trust for people who deliberately cover up crimes against human life. Could you feel really confident in their ability to make decisions that reflect globally on a population that's entitled to have honest, responsible people working in government positions that service the population's needs? What to do when the system enables its "leaders" to abdicate responsibility for their misdeeds and permits one group of bums to vacate office with impunity, to be replaced by another group voted in by a disillusioned constituency hoping for change?

Two young males murdered by members of our clan and we are each stained by the disgrace. Imagine the anguish their mothers suffer *that never goes away*, the grief and the feelings of vulnerability that hit their community when its sons were *killed* by foreign militarists.

End of story, even though it goes on. Except. Suppose, just suppose for a minute that Shidane Arone had been a sixteen-year-old blue-eyed Canadian youth who was horribly murdered by "dark fellows" from an African nightmare force? And further, suppose the murdered youngster was named Art Eggleton Junior?

Is it true that it begins with the desire rather than a thought to create change for change to ultimately be?

So I'm in Victoria visiting with my friend Constable Keith the Cop and the discussion gets around to the United States being an armed camp. Although we agree the world would be a far better place if there were no guns, we have different views about the individual's right to own a gun. Americans, I feel, honor each individual's right to own guns, regardless of what judgements we entertain about the ugly purpose of those cursed things. Constable Keith, with one of those black semi automatics strapped on his side, stands strong on the argument that people shouldn't be allowed to own guns and I agreed. But darnit, it didn't occur to me until after I left his precinct to ask why Constable Keith had a gun and why I shouldn't be allowed to have one, all things being equal. But then, they're not equal, are they?

There's an attitude that goes with owning a gun and an even more potent attitude that goes with owning a gun, wearing it strapped to your uniformed body and being able to get away with shooting a hole in someone with a bullet from that gun. In the thinking of more and more people cops getting away with shooting folks is a valid reason to secure for themselves by any means possible the tools that support being free from the intimidating effects of unequal distribution of that kind of power. Consider how the situation changes when the guy who's had the only gun in town wakes up one morning to learn that everyone else got a gun too. Better that there were no guns for everyone.

You Must Think You're As Good As I Am

I'll bet I'm not the only person who's lost jobs in Canada and been given to feel like the villain. My first firing occurred at a major advertising agency in Toronto, where I had transferred from the American parent company I was happily doing well at. A year later I was gone, the first time a member of my family was ever dismissed from a job.

My supervisor had been an adult immigrant from South Africa. The client we serviced had an arsenic attitude toward Americans and he didn't expend an ounce to diffuse his ugly feelings about ad material being produced in the States and modified for Canadian content—stepchild advertising, he felt. One of the execs on a beer account, a man named Snetsinger, referred to folks like me as "you guys" as though we were from a place that could never qualify for acceptance. This man had a way of calling us "negroes" that could make you think we were half naked splayfoot buffoons. On one occasion he placed his soft pink fingertips on my lustrous Afro hair like my hair was steel wool pricklies and hissed an exaggerated *"Owwch!"*

Although it was subtly expressed, I knew unquestionably that I wasn't "one of the guys," except among some of the oppressed other class: women. What can a guy do in a situation like that? I was the only non-Caucasoid person in that Toronto, Ontario advertising agency, isolated and lonely among men who were ignorant, and resistant to even the concept of exploring cultural understanding. They didn't have to.

Next I thought I had been hired by a major Canadian-owned agency that didn't first confer with its client, a major United States-owned automotive manufacturer doing business in Canada. During lunch the two men I was scheduled to begin work with told me that a threat to the business relationship loomed if the agency placed a "negro" (can you imagine?) on the account. Sorry, they apologized, we hope you understand.

I don't understand. But thanks for your honesty, gentlemen. Somehow I don't believe I can bring myself to buy another of your client's products for as long as I live. However, because it would be an injustice to their growing process I wouldn't infect my offspring with their father's experience and the kids may some day become your client's customers. It's inevitable and history confirms that within bastions of resistance to progress there'll ultimately be a changing of the guard and with it a change in the way we do business with each other.

The agency? McLaren Advertising. The automotive manufacturer? General Motors. The two messengers? Bill Vernon and Jerry Scarfe.

(A weakness in out nature moves us to deny or to strike back when our bellies are exposed. Suppose that step was bypassed and some fair-minded, evolved person engaged in, "Hey, let's check into it with motivation to seeing this never happens in our place again")

While visiting Red Walter in Los Angeles I connected with some folks who hired me in L.A. to work in their Toronto office. After six months I managed to push an increase of the media budget on one account from $40,000 to just over $200,000 based primarily on the results of a study that revealed extraordinary French Canadian consumption of their citrus product. We found out that essentially for health reasons French Canadian moms treated their children to citrus products rather than sugar-based things that poison the system and turn young teeth into problems. So engaged in the process was I it didn't register that I had activated a delicate nerve in the Canadian male psyche: a dark-skinned foreigner cultivating business in an area they had neglected through cultural ignorance.

Finally, my supervisor on a different retail account, a man threatened by the rapport that developed between myself and the ad manager of an account we jointly serviced, got rid of me, fired me off'n the job, put my butt in the unemployment line and do you have any *idea* how hard it is to cop a gig in Canada if you're not one of the boys?

Bill was distemperoid with insecurity. He had accused me of sleeping with our secretary. He ordered me to discontinue the occasional Friday client meeting in the park on a sunny day with a bottle of cabernet, disposable wine glasses and tasty deli food, where we casually worked on business and tossed bite-size chunks to little feathered things with wings. During those afternoons the gentleman ad client and the ad agency account guy invariably got a lot of good done and parted with a smiling handshake after having communicated more during a few warm hours outdoors than we could have in any glassed-in setting.

Bill, who usually brown-bagged it and ate in his office with his feet up and the door closed, would select a favorite upscale restaurant for client lunches. During one of these engagements the client and I picked up where we had left off from our previous meeting, inadvertently omitting Bill, which moved Bill to splash a handful of change on the table and command me to "Go feed the meter."

Whoops. Hey bud, it's your money, your car, your mistake and this is an act that plays just once.

The final indiscretion hit when a group of us collected at a popular side-street drinking spot and Mister Bill, after stringing out some strategically sequenced marginal comments, took the step into telling me to go to the bar and fetch him a beer.

Whoops again, pal.

With Bill continuing to smile in my face like everything was hunky-dory I had no idea that consequences would tally up to being told it was time to leave again. I say that I had no idea but I think a deeper truth is that I did know, otherwise I wouldn't have accepted my role in the game, which was equal parts Bill and myself. That we tuned in to each other's stuff and validated that stuff through our actions—*Stop it, boys!*—placed us both smack dab in the middle of tit for tat.

Finally, I felt humbled to my ankles when I applied for an advertising position at 3M in London, Ontario. The feeling expressed was *How dare you even think to apply for a job like this!* and I was all but run off the property, my ego, which was weak to begin with, bashed and any idealism I had brought with me from the States dashed. Not knowing better at the time I bought the lie and of all the choices available I opted to go down, down, down. Completing a slide that had started years earlier I released to a mechanism that allowed me to slide into po' me. In that process I attached to defeatist feelings, alcohol and other numbing agents, becoming in the doing an accomplice in the assassination of my own spirit.

It ain't how many times you fall down, Richard Bud, it's how many times you get up.

A popular Toronto executive search person had coached me to look for a stock room job or leave the city. He laughed good-naturedly and said, "You thought you were as good as them, you asshole." Years later a female health care executive in Portland, Oregon would say that the situation was about *I am who I am* interacting with *I am what I do.*

Ironically, I did both of what the Toronto guy suggested, leaving Tranna to find work for a while in the London, Ontario warehouse of the Murphy Tobacco Company.

My Canada. That was back in the early nineteen seventies. We're into the next century and progress is little more than a word, an illusion, an out of-its-element snail dehydrating. Back in the 1960s Dr. Chatters had counseled me to "Go to the United States and fulfill your potential. Americans invest in their people. Canadians drain their workers like leeches sucking out your life's essence. You would not be happy under the power of men who refuse to know who you are and who don't want to know you as anything other than a stereotyped object." Also, I would have access to constitutional rights that originated in the soul of a republic rather than paper rights "awarded" to one of mother's stepchildren. How could anyone validate the notion that another can grant or refuse something—your *free*dom—you were *born* with?

So I went back to the States and worked hourly jobs for temporary agencies while I worked out what to do with my life, recovering, as my friend Wally Dalton observed, from my Canadian experience.

On my first assignment to a major banking institution the man I reported to casually reviewed with me what had to be done, asked if I was clear on his instructions and then left me in that bank office to do the job. Jotting down his cell phone number he said, "If you need any help, call me. Otherwise I'll see you

tomorrow. Take your time and I hope you have a good night."
I felt good right from the beginning with this man, who is Roger
Langdon. We started with respect for one another as individual
human beings who came together to accomplish a task. This with
the understanding that a liberated spirit will creatively, joyfully,
freely and with confidence execute the assigned responsibilities
because, you see, it's not the task that's important, it's the people
doing the task who are important. *Here are your duties, my friend,
and I have unqualified confidence in your ability to do the best
possible job. If you need support let me know.*

May I Please?

Because we occasionally explore different routes to arrive at a specific location, my teenage son and I elected to take the U.S.-based private enterprise ship MV Coho, which sails between downtown Victoria, British Columbia and Port Angeles, Washington. It's a relatively short hour and thirty-some minute trip followed by a drive of several hours on a two-lane thoroughfare to Bremerton and a Washington State Ferries trip to Seattle.

When we arrived at the Bremerton terminal I paid at the tollbooth and pulled into a line of only a few cars, which meant it was a beginning line and we had some waiting time. "Look!" Jess exclaimed, "We're surrounded by a city. Let's go buy some goodies from a store."

I thought briefly about his response to something I hadn't noticed. Then my mind traveled back to Victoria and conditions involved in taking a British Columbia Ferries Corporation vessel. We had to drive almost twenty miles along a highway where you could be pretty sure there would be police photo-radar traps, pay our toll at Swartz Bay and pull into a line as directed. If we failed to follow the directions we would be reminded over a loud speaker system. We were fenced in, had access to only one food service, that of the British Columbia Ferries Corporation. From the instant we paid our toll we were under B.C. Ferries Corporation control. Conditioning may therefore have been at the source of responding to the kid's enthusiasm with, "Let's check in with the toll taker first."

"No problem," the toll taker responded with a casual friendliness that involved patting my arm. "Your only restriction is time and you got at least forty-five minutes before the next boat." The man was bubbling with goodwill. I realized that there were no fences containing us and no speaker system belching in the background. "Thanks," I responded and started to walk away.

"Hey, come back here for a minute," he called, which I did with questioning eyebrows. "You're from Canada, aren't you."

I asked if he had noticed our British Columbia car plates.

"Uh-uh."

"Is it the way I talk?"

"Nope."

"Then how could you know?"

"Because," he laughed, "you had to ask for permission."

The Best Things In Life Aren't Things

Adjusting to a materialistic lifestyle doesn't work for me and I don't feel the need to fault that it does work for others. I don't believe that personal value is measured by net worth. Relationships based on class, as determined by what one owns—things—or what one does to earn money as opposed to people opening to one another simply because they breathe the same air.

I'll always feel refreshed by the next person who expresses genuine interest in who I am.

Beautiful blond-haired P-Girl is best friends with someone who's been known to ask male Victorians, "How long have you been dead?" It's based on people who come through with a lifeless "Na bad" or "Na too bad" in responding to, "How are you?" Beautiful blond-haired P-Girl observed also that people who come back with "Na bad" or "Na too bad" usually fail to return the courtesy with, "And how are you?"

Na too bad, eh?

Backtracking

This narrative connects with three relationships that led to understanding how an entrenched social process influenced an alien son's perceptions as a romance seeker. Sometimes the most elusive concepts to git aholt to are those we bin tooken inside, those that become as much a part of who believe we are as breathing in and breathing out.

Let's move the calendar to the mid 1990s and my chronological age to the mid fifties. Assume I'm a fairly intelligent, moderately appealing male who doesn't suffer from melanin deprivation. I value women in the way of one who's been programmed to objectify these lovely creatures but finally am evolving into an appreciation of female beings for the value they present. Not yet in that place where I'm developing an awareness of missed opportunities to see someone for who they were due to my agenda at the time, but moving in that direction. Because sex was a factor in previous relationships sex was still significant until this process.

Before moving to the city of Victoria, British Columbia, a quaint mutation of an imaginary Mother England that's named after a dead British ruler, I had been jumping around like a restless frog hopping from lily pad to lily pad. I was emotionally numbed to the deeper experience of coming together with someone, as well as being depressed by the hopelessness that's at the bottom of feeling controlled. Searching outside when my answers were inside. Then, after attempts to connect with spirits who became friends or part of the past, I encountered a woman who invited me to sit with her at a Yates Street coffee shop one afternoon. We talked about what we did rather than who we were and I got the impression she was impressed that she was a lawyer. "Are you a lawyer," I asked, "or a woman who practices the law?" For the briefest instant she bristled but recovered with a certain poise and said, "I'm a woman who practices the law." Too bad she was on her way somewhere else to do something else she added, giving me her business card and hurrying along.

Being fairly new to Victoria she hadn't yet become affected by the class structuring and we became close. Our spirits tried to connect, briefly experiencing touches but not opening to sharing our unprotected selves when we weren't being physically intimate. We came from different teachings, different understandings and beliefs. We were actually two different couples. We projected one image for the benefit of outsiders, an image determined by conservative social expectations: who we were expected to be. I can only be who I am, Biggety. Ultimately we struggled with conflicting values. Our inner children engaged in stubbornness. We attacked each other's shame. The relationship couldn't survive.

Next I was gifted with a medical person whose physical beauty touched me only slightly less than her unawareness of how lovely a person she was. She invited me to her Oak Bay home, a stylish structure outfitted with multiple fireplaces, pastel walls hosting modest original art and a kitchen equipped with designer appliances, where she served shrimp and French white wine. As our evening ended I felt flattered when the lady suggested visiting me sometime.

Driving across town in my old Volvo station wagon I started feeling progressively more tense and by the time my feet crossed the front doorway I was so stressed that I had to restrain myself from telephoning her and saying, "Look, I don't want you coming to my house and I don't want to see you again," which wasn't even close to what I wanted.

What the hell was going on with me? I looked around my living room, trying to get a handle on the fear that displaced my anticipation of seeing her. My house was clean, neat, tidy, situated on a treed street of well-kept dwellings. On recently painted white walls were framed photos of people I loved, creative art prints and vinegar-clean windows that allowed the sun to create beauty with hanging stained glass pieces I had commissioned. *What, I thought, am I so terrified of?*

Being rejected. The answer flashed in my mind like a neon bolt. *Rejected?* I needed to bring what the answer meant a little further along, from the emotional me through the steps to putting my mind around it. *Why am I afraid this woman will reject me?* I scanned my environment again. Couldn't be that. *Is it because she's a doctor?* No. I see her as a woman, not as a doctor. *Then what is it?* A process had started that I didn't identify. *Have I ever felt that way about American women?* Not really, but American women were different. Most American women were pretty up front in their actions. It seemed to me they were aggressive, more open, less shame-based. *Then how about European women?* Never. Europeans I had experienced looked beyond the shell to whatever it was about the inner person that spoke to them. *Okay, if that's the case I need to figure out why Canadian women trigger this damn fear in me.*

I reviewed every relationship I could recall, beginning with my lawyer friend. What had this particular female done that didn't activate the roadblocks one accrues in the rejection process? Well, the woman approved me. She indicated that I was okay in her eyes. She gave me permission. A common thread, I discovered, in my relationships with Canadian females as I traveled back through years of personal history. *There's no fear of being rejected when someone else initiates contact.* How far back did my memory take me to reach that place of seeing? The trip back carried me to the school we were transferred to after Mercer Street School burned down during my kindergarten year.

Mercer Street School had been our ghetto gathering place for learning, a place where we played freely and practiced the unqualified love kids just put out there for one another. Mercer Street School was in the heart of our community; it was a center of love and growth. When a fire took that precious institution from us the lower McDougall Street kids were obliged to attend Frank W. Begley elementary school, situated in a working class area. Some of our new schoolmates felt that we were lower than rat droppings because people who are deprived and/or who live inside a dark outer shell are alien undesirables in the eyes of the unenlightened. To many but certainly not all of them we were creatures to avoid. So, because we had played in the Mercer Street school yard as a mixture of kids who weren't yet exposed to the effects of being from another element in the social scheme we naturally expected that Frank W. Begley would be the same fulfilling experience, schoolyards being schoolyards and kids being kids.

In my experience Canadian bigots are in most cases not given to blatantly assigning labels like "nigger," I would suggest because the Canadian way is to subtly *treat* someone in the manner they believe a "nee-gair" or other "lesser" being requires being treated.

It's obscene life theatre that both parties—the sender and the receiver—are involuntarily sucked into because that's the way life is in this time and place and a little person's mind isn't conscious of being absorbed into the process. They may sense that what's forming inside isn't for the good of all while being incapable of stopping the program from taking root in their fertile psyches. The roles they're assigned—*I am this and you are that. We are different and I am privileged,* is complemented on the other side by the belief that *I am that and you are this. We're different and I am less.* This tragic understanding is reinforced at every step along their paths by parents, in the media, in literature & folklore, in the classroom and in the actions of the general population. Again, that's the way life is in this time and place and as far as they know it's a true story that life will forever be that way.

That belief sticks like chewing gum in the sidewalk sun. Like the stunning beauty who lived a lifetime and died believing she was an unlovable duckling because people who influenced her childhood said her feet were big and her nose was an unsightly knob. Even though she grew into a delight to the sight, being defined as an Ugly Duckling set her up for a life of plunge-quickies and difficult serial relationships.

Ever seeking, never fulfilling.

As receivers of class-based rejection by scrubbed schoolgirls who didn't know any better we were prey to a feeling—*We don't like you around us; you're not acceptable. You're distasteful. You're not good enough!*—that demeaned, degraded, disenfranchised and dehumanized.

In order to see the picture the way it was hung it took a relation-ship with an aggressive lawyer and a non-intimate exploration of friendship with a gentle physician to detect and then translate internalized fear into understanding. A release from being yesterday's child victim in today's adult world? Feeling ugly, inadequate, undesirable, unqualified, unwanted and alien without knowing why is a place many have lived in, some without relief.

The third person I was presented with was significant in that she became someone the emotional me was sufficiently released from uncertainty shackles to approach in a public setting and to later open my heart to. Ironically, the lady was a counselor.

Hey Kiefer, if life is a big process are there myriad little processes within it?

Rudolph the Red Nosed Reindeer was discriminated against because the color of his nose was different.

We would do well to put our differences in the past, grow from experiences we share and share experiences we create.

I regret that I've been deeply bitter, angry and driven at times by intense rage. It was a waste. At times during a tumultuous past I tried to pound Caucasian men (many) into bloody pulp with rage-driven balled-up fists, and to sexually con– quer Caucasian women (none). I succeeded only in depriving myself of genuinely getting to know another person or, worse, of not even seeing them *as* a person. At no time was I conscious of what I was doing; I became a driven someone I wasn't born to be, a total, un– reasoning racist reactionary who blamed the outer world for my inner turmoil. *You made me what I am!* And yes, like my frustrated father I chose to rage at my loved ones, with none of us possessing the slightest notion why Daddy could become so volatile. We didn't know how to interpret the message behind the rage: *I am oppressed and I hate this feeling, I hate being treated as less and I hate feeling helpless to do anything short of violence to change it. I hate being treated like an intruder, like some kind of villain.* It was obvious to anyone looking in that I didn't possess the tools I needed to turn myself to peacefully changing things within myself rather than reacting wildly like an enraged, wounded bull.

Had I bought the program, I mean did I fit into it like we were meant for each other?

My friend Bill Johnstone, a liberal and caring Canadian of Scottish ancestry, challenged me about the bitterness I produced based on my experience with the Canadian Establishment and I apologized to Bill because he seemed to take it personally as an attack on his country. But later the emotional me mailed a letter saying, in essence, "Who are you to criticize my feelings about the way 'your Canada' has treated me and people like me?" My Canada and his Canada are different. Although people like Bill can be held in place by fear—neutralized from bringing out what they feel within, including their position in opposition to the threat against openly expressing one's true self, they enjoy relative privilege. Bill is an Insider. But the rascal still needs to pay rent and buy food, which means he's one in a cast of masses who are vulnerable to our old companions Power, Fear and Control. Even so, Bill can get and go to a job interview with the confidence that "By Jove, Old Boy…" isn't a concealed obstruction (neither in his reality nor in his fears) to his application.

It could be that through the effects of alienation I no longer permit myself to be intimidated by that threat, have not allowed something as relatively insignificant (yet essential) as a job to influence the valuing of my fundamental rights. I must admit, however, to a disabling fear of being vulnerable in that arena again. Because I've had jobs taken from me I've experienced the tragedy of being unable to provide for my family and I've struggled with the emptiness that accompanies being cast out. No matter what I tell myself it's a place I never want to be in again.

This affirms a commitment to voicing the understanding that Canada is a systemically racist, a culturally ignorant nation. That racism, like sexism, should be *against the law* and that bureaucrats on every level are *individually accountable* for the damage that racism and related "isms" are allowed to inflict. There simply has to be a dismantling of the systems traditionally maintained by White Anglo Saxon men and passed into the stewardship of others like them. By its nature this greedy, self-satisfying practice deprives others, facilitating a hopelessness that fosters drunkenness, addiction, depression and spiritual death. That, to me, is criminal.

Do you think the basics in this authority-based governing system can use some updating, Albert? Maybe a wee bit of change? Can Canadians allow themselves to at least consider looking more closely at the example of their neighboring republic and maybe by seeing from the outside improve on mistakes that occur during that system's process? Keeping in mind that the independent country grew by huge proportions compared to the colony that was held in check (goldfished), both are young turks that can align/combine to create growth that's simply unimaginable. Imagine. Canadian-style medicine introducing balance and not-for-profit caring into the U.S. medical field. Medicine from the heart like it's practiced in Cuba. Now, *that* would be something, do you think, Hillary?

Americans for the most part are co-operative, mostly caring people, independent spirits who don't seek permission to exercise their freedom. They're folks who'll make an individual decision to cross the street on a red light simply because no traffic is in sight, people who aren't programmed to surrender to a controlling "authority" that demands they request permission and obey. Do this or else, eh what? For God's sake, in Canada the controls are so tight that you almost have to get permission to think and even then, Sister, be careful who you express your thoughts to.

Controlling people isn't respecting them. Controlling people is feeding an unnatural need for power over them. When was life meant to be *that* way?

You know what's good for you and I know what's good for me. Let's get together and decide what's good for us.

When we stop regarding each other as threats a way clears for us to join together as One.

Who are you?

anada's time to develop its own identity is like a payment to one's personal account that's long past due. If folks took time to look inward they could open to one another and see how far we're able to move ahead together. What if we set ourselves free to be who we are in the purest sense and in the doing create the cohesiveness we're capable of? Suppose we support each other like family members while we're on the path? It makes so much more sense for us to accept each other, period. That's how I'd like to see my Canada, a progressive republic of freely relating people, indivisible and committed to transforming yesterday's learning opportunities into today's forward motion. There's nothing we can't do and everything we can accomplish together.

Free yourself.

When I sat down to do this somewhere in my mind was a thought that "This is my story!" but having finished I know this isn't any one person's story. I realized this one afternoon while working as a movie extra in *Men of Courage* when a young University of Oregon student from Zimbabwe and I chatted about our experiences. As it happened we both had the experience of being raised in a land that had been raped by the same invader. (Why is it that if one human rapes another it's a violation but when one country rapes another it's a victory?)

I realized then that what's true for Canada is also true for India, Asian nations, Australia, New Zealand, Ireland, Brazil and so many others that were violated by sick, greedy people from Britain, France, Japan, Spain, Portugal, the Netherlands, China and now the United States with megadollar power that can gobble up a nation more effectively than bullets and bombs.

When will the madness end?

NOTES/COMMENTS/THOUGHTS

I'm deeply interested in your comments
and, if you wish to share them, any experiences
that reading this may have brought back.
Please be free to reach me by writing to
Post Office Box 86034, Portland, Oregon 97286.
Thank you for reading this material.

ISBN 155212706-0

9 781552 127063